ETHICS OF
VACCINE PASSPORTS:
A Poor Bargain

ETHICS OF
VACCINE PASSPORTS:
A Poor Bargain

Aviel Oppenheim

ISBN: 978-1-7387151-1-4

For family,

who make it all possible.

Contents

Part IV: Constitutionality

Part V: Epilogue

"If we wish to preserve a free society, it is essential that we recognize that the desirability of a particular object is not sufficient justification for the use of coercion."

F.A. Hayek

Part I:
The Preface

Chapter 1

WHAT HAPPENED?

A tyranny sincerely exercised for the good of its victims may be the most oppressive... those who torment us for our own good will torment us without end, for they do so with the approval of their own conscience.

C.S. Lewis[1]

The years between 2020 and 2022 were an unprecedented time in human history. The extent to which governments invaded the private lives of individuals transformed society into a blend between the realities of George Orwell's *1984*, Aldous Huxley's *Brave New World*, and Alan Moore's *V for Vendetta*. We need no longer peer as far back as the twentieth century for potent examples to the nature of totalitarianism and authoritarian governance.

In the beginning of 2020, governments around the world assumed absolute *emergency powers* that have yet to be completely relinquished two years and counting. Their excuse was an airborne virus; a virus the government deemed threatening enough to justify their own expansion. A virus that was supposedly so deadly, that they fined and arrested anyone who left their home or were in physical proximity to someone of another household. To reiterate, the virus was so dangerous that citizens were held at gunpoint by their governments. The police-state that formed in the year 2020, in response to SARS-CoV-2, a coronavirus associated with the infectious disease referred to as covid-19, has similarly yet to be relinquished two years and counting. With the dictate of "international authority," lockdowns, compulsory face coverings, and forced physical distancing mandates spread throughout the globe in complete harmony. It was as though a memo had been forwarded to every government body demanding all nations sing to the same tune. The official narrative was to hibernate, with the threat of fines and imprisonment, and await a vaccine; a vaccine that would be wielded as a stick to an obedient dog.

The largest pharmaceutical companies in the world conjured up a vaccine at the end of 2020, and governments mantled the will of tyranny, cloaked under the guise of safety, and set an ultimatum with its people. The ultimatum was to accept a pharmaceutical product or be subjected to further lockdowns and restrictions. In other words, people were compelled to do as the government said or be locked away and barred from human interaction and the means to survive. As to be expected with any use of government force, there were citizens who complied and those who dissented. The people who refused were locked up in their homes, barred from employment, and ostracized from all facets of ordinary society. Those who complied were similarly locked up and restricted, albeit granted more privileges than their counterparts. A notable difference between the two camps, however, was that the obedient blamed their cage not on the government that threw away the key, but on their own neighbours who were caged all the same. And some did not only blame but fear their neighbours. They feared the breath of others and the very biological, *germ-infested* existence of their own species. For the first time in history, breathing felt like a criminal offense.

This fear among the masses spread like wildfire and became so potent – stoked by government and their propagandized communications – that people seemed all too content to live the rest of their lives in the new cage they were given; faceless and confined. The fear corrupted the human psyche so intimately that many outright advocated for their friends and family to be locked away in their homes indefinitely. The fear-stricken masses were placed under a spell to believe, wholeheartedly, that their sacrifice of liberty was in the name of the deity known as *public health*. A remarkable and frightening blend of germophobic paranoia and passivity to government intrusion permeated 2020 and the two years that followed.

On the eve of 2022, nothing had changed except for the addition of vaccine passports, which were introduced globally months prior. The inevitable consequence of the government's ultimatum, between freedom and the acceptance of a pharmaceutical injection, was a passport to distinguish the compliers from the dissenters. A passport that rewarded the "privilege" of liberty to those who obeyed and punished any who had refused, redefining their liberties as a privilege to be taken away. Vaccine passports ensured that people who refused the government's decree were to be labeled as the "unvaccinated" and placed in perpetual lockdowns and restrictions. This was considered the appropriate treatment towards those who were made into second-class citizens as a result of their differing vaccination status. The years between 2020 and 2021 were alas marked by lockdowns, mandates, and vaccine passports around the globe. It was a period to be remembered as the subjugation of the human existence to imprisonment-compelled obedience. While the government's *philanthropic tyranny* woke up countless individuals who harbored a naïve trust in the State, the government's expansion during its *war on covid* was coupled by an unprecedented display of collectivist support. A display of support towards government expansion that paralleled the fascist, or state-corporatist, movements of the early twentieth century.

While 2022 began in the footsteps of its predecessor, the government's invasion into the private lives of individuals waned in the following months throughout most of the world, including Canada – the place I reside. This long-overdue abdication was a result of the demonstrative failure of government intervention towards covid-19 and the overarching failure of the "war on covid." It seemed that time had caught up with governments who enjoyed their authoritarianism and consequently overstayed their welcome, at least in the west. The governments who spearheaded lockdowns and mandates finally encountered more backlash from the populace they lorded over and imprisoned the last two years.

The war on covid proved ineffective to prevent the fluctuating highs of covid transmission. People were still getting sick with cold and flu-like symptoms, which perplexed those who believed themselves capable of eradicating the nature of sickness. In 2022, governments around the world consequently shifted their approach and, instead, called for everyone to "learn to live with covid-19." Humorously, this scaling-back rhetoric was adopted at a time when covid cases were far higher than they were the prior two years. It was expected that governments would inevitably take the knife off the neck of their citizens at an arbitrary place and time. It was over when the State said so, and when it said so was when it was most politically beneficial.

Throughout 2020 and 2021, people all over world including Canadians were not allowed to live with a virus and the disease of covid-19. They were caged to avoid it. In the year 2022, however, ordinary individuals were arbitrarily given permission, from their wardens, to resume their lives normally once again. This permission slip of normality has alas proved to be likely temporary. In the summer of 2022, the World Health Organization (WHO) declared that covid-19 remained "a public health emergency of international concern," which has invited countries to declare their seventh and eighth "waves" in response to seasonal case fluctuations and politically expedient "variants of concern." The European Union also extended its legal framework for vaccine passports into 2023, offering some unfortunate insights into the future ahead.

It remains to be seen the extent to which governments will revitalize their efforts once more. What I am certain of, however, is that governments bestowed upon themselves the power they wielded throughout these last two years. Thus, those who have arbitrarily rescinded their power are just as likely to arbitrarily grant themselves that power again. With that said, I have waited long enough before publishing this book to those who ought to read it most. If I waited for the government-covid hysteria to fade into history, and for all its doors to close, it is unlikely this book would ever be read.

The reality of the present is complex; the events that have led us to this day are unprecedented and worthy of historical documentation. Such events ought to also be subjected to extensive and scathing critique. In bringing to light the dystopia that plagued the world between 2020-2022, my aim is to explore the dreadful creation of vaccine passports: a malevolent measure concocted by government in their war against covid-19. By illuminating the dark reality of vaccine passports, the book holds accountable both the governments that implemented them and the people who advocated its use.

Chapter 2

INTRODUCTION

A prominent American broadcaster by the name of Edward R. Murrow made a heartfelt plea, in 1954, that read the following:

"We will not walk in fear, of one another. We will not be driven by fear into an age of unreason...remember that we are not descended from fearful men. Not from men who feared to write, to speak, to associate, and to defend causes that were, for the moment, unpopular."[1]

I humbly borrow the words of the late Edward Murrow, for there is no greater time than the present to utter them once more. As I look around today, I fear humanity has once again reached the precipice of a world consumed by fear. It was the rise of vaccine passports and its rapid State-propagated enforcement and normalization that led me to the urgent moral need to write these subsequent thoughts onto paper. Prior to the year 2020, I had no such plans to ever write this book. Akin to the experience of others, 2020 and the two years that followed charted a new path for which I felt morally obliged to traverse. In the spirit of Mr. Murrow, I ought to defend a cause that is today unpopular as to ensure it may yet be popular tomorrow; similarly, I intend to critique what is today popular so that it may be unpopular tomorrow. It is first paramount to mention that a vaccine passport is a euphemism for a *societal freedom passport*; both its nature and function are identical. This euphemism is made more apparent throughout the book. In acknowledging the nature of vaccine passports, it will also become easier to understand why such a creation was never on the conscience of most people until the year 2020. Unfortunately, now its rhetoric is so commonplace it may seem as though it has always existed.

For many, vaccine passports were a nightmare that others told them had always existed in some form – that there was nothing far-fetched about them. Some were even tempted to ponder why it took so long for their implementation. How could one have lived so long never being reassured of the vaccine history of their surroundings, they asked themselves. These convenient newfound revelations and rationalizations, moulded at the sight of covid-19, were largely the result of government propaganda broadcasted towards a populace primed to passively adhere to the ultimate form of authority: government, or the State.

With the onslaught of fear and paranoia, the populace was conditioned to accept the idea that vaccine passports were not only the key to have their lives back but the key to freedom itself. While some may not have deliberately done so, the advocacy for vaccine passports more broadly normalized the notion of *freedom passports*. Supporters of vaccine passports quantified liberty like was never done before. It went beyond the scope of colour and ethnicity, and it indiscriminately affected anyone who dared disobey government decree or the orders of pharmaceutical executives. The existence of a freedom passport, based on the acceptance of a pharmaceutical injection, should be a nightmare for any individual. It should be of concern particularly to those that care for their own liberty and that of their family, peers, and those who will be *excommunicated* for resisting.

A family that was split on vaccine passports were divided not only ideologically, but physically in their own backyards. A father who was unvaccinated was unable to enter a restaurant with his son; an unvaccinated mother was unable to enter entertain a theatre with her daughter; an uncle who was unvaccinated was barred from traveling to a nephew's birthday party; and an unvaccinated brother was prohibited from entering campus to visit his sister. The reality that came to fruition between 2020-2022 was, by definition, an apartheid. It was government-enforced segregation cloaked under the premise of philanthropy.

I have been compelled to manifest my voice into these inked letters as to bring reason to those who have never sat down and, while putting aside their fears, ever pondered the existence and implications of a vaccine passport. That is, what the requirement to show government-issued vaccination proof to enter a café says about the nature of humanity, freedom, and government. I do not doubt that there were those who, in their misguidance, supported vaccine passports without realizing the extremity to which they upended fundamental conceptions intrinsically linked to the human race.

A domestic vaccine passport is a government document that identifies your vaccination status, which is used to regulate and dictate what ordinary life activities you are allowed to partake in. By way of forcing everyone, including employers and landowners, to demand proof of vaccination, vaccine passports prohibit individuals from societal or ordinary life without the display of their vaccination status – either due to a refusal to vaccinate or a refusal to show proof. The vaccine passports for covid-19 that swept the world were in essence a barcode that, while traditionally would have been tattooed on bodily skin, was printed upon a digital screen. A technological advancement that symbolized the *progressive* times of the twenty-first century. The notion of requiring a vaccine passport to live ordinary life, such as to enter a café, was once unheard of. Alas, in the span of a fortnight the idea became normalized globally.

It is important to emphasize that domestic vaccine passports stripped freedoms away not only from the unvaccinated, but from those who refused to disclose their vaccination status. In the eye of the State, the person who refused the vaccine and the person who declined to show proof of vaccination had in common a simple thing: a refusal to show allegiance. The vaccinated who refused to play along with vaccine passports were penalized, akin to the un-vaccinated, for not conforming to the dictate of government man-date. They were penalized the same because they were innately pre-sumed to be *unvaccinated* and thus treated accordingly. As you read along, the connection between vaccine passports and State alle-giance will become more apparent.

My book explores the moral, scientific, and legal notions, conse-quences, and implications of vaccine passports so as to demonstrate its dehumanizing nature and negative impact on the fabric of humanity. Through its multifaceted analysis, the book notably chronicles the global use of vaccine passports and the overarching crusade against covid-19. This piece of writing may therefore stand as a cautionary tale of accepting vaccine passports into human society; a tale that ends with a society that walks in fear of one another, lest it even be called *human* anymore.

Part II:
What Gave Rise to Vaccine Passports

Chapter 3

GOVERNMENT-INDUCED COMPLIANCE

> *The belief that there is only one right way to live, only one right way to regulate religious, political, sexual, [and] medical affairs is the root cause of the greatest threat to man: members of his own species, bent on ensuring his salvation, security, and sanity.*

Thomas Szasz[1]

To better understand why vaccine passports are morally abhorrent, it is first important to address what facets of society and everyday life enabled its existence. After all, the masses must have been conditioned to suddenly tolerate and advocate for a life controlled and regulated by vaccine passports. Given the need for this foundational context, the following two chapters address the psychological and social matrix that has permeated the perception towards vaccines. It is this matrix, or distorted mass-perception, which is the likely culprit that subverted a populace to accept what surmounted to a freedom passport. In other words, we must first come to understand both the fervent defense of vaccines, to all forms of critique, and the cultist obsession with vaccine uniformity and compliance. This devotion to vaccine uniformity did not spring up spontaneously with the arrival of covid-19; it had fermented for generations prior. It was only in 2020, at the signal of government health officials, that this uniformity blossomed into robotic obedience.

The militant and government-mobilized promotion and defense of covid vaccinations both contributed to, and exposed, the vaccine orthodoxy and the taboo surrounding vaccine criticism. Government institutions and ministries actively advocated for, and defended, the covid vaccination campaign. In doing so, the State limited any information or human conduct that hindered their objective. Supporters of vaccine passports, who were the fervent defenders of the government's vaccination campaign, also labeled "dangerous" any information that bred skepticism towards covid vaccines. This general notion that critiquing vaccines is dangerous and harmful is precisely the foundation that turned a populace passive in response to a covid vaccination crusade. A crusade that suppressed any unconventional viewpoints or beliefs towards covid vaccines and government intervention branded under the label of "public health." A suppression that opened the door to arguably the most dystopian government mandate of all: vaccine passports.

COVID VACCINE CRUSADE

The covid vaccine crusade was a global campaign that was set on vaccinating the entire world so as to fell the *dragon* of covid-19. The crusading was blatant and overt in the government-corporate media, however it extended to every facet of ordinary society. Outside of the sweeping government vaccine mandates and passports that ostracized unvaccinated citizens both socially and financially, State institutions and bedded corporate entities contributed more subtly to the injustice that coerced millions to accept a pharmaceutical product.

The Occupational Safety and Health Administration (OSHA), a large regulatory agency of the United States Department of Labor, did not enforce workplaces compelled to require covid vaccination to report vaccine related side effects or fatalities. Their reason was that "it would dissuade others from vaccinating."[2] In other words, a government agency omitted the truth because it conflicted with the government's mission. To make matters worse, the OSHA was the government body responsible for executing the federal vaccine mandate for workplaces throughout the United States.

A government institution, created in the name of health and safety, forced workers to consent to medical injections under duress while ensuring any resulting injuries were censored. It might seem ironic, that an agency predicated upon safety and health would embody such Orwellian contradictions. This doublethink, however, does not surprise the keen observer. It is the inevitable conclusion when governments are given reign to monopolize what health and safety means to every individual. Whether or not you personally perceive health and safety differently is irrelevant; government officials know best, and you need only obey. This centralized monopoly on health and safety is the foundation that enabled governments to implement lockdowns and mandates by the mere wave of their hand. A feat no ordinary citizen would be granted the legitimacy, or militant prowess, to implement and enforce. Alas, government bureaucrats are equipped, and treated, far more *lavishly*.

On the theme of omitting truth in the name of ulterior objectives, a stapled principle of the covid vaccination crusade, social media platforms pioneered censorship campaigns to spearhead their contributions to the cause. And they made their contributions in deceptive collaboration with governments. With the arrival of the government's war on covid, the largest social media platforms, in synchronized fashion, updated their terms of services in accordance with the official narrative of the State. In an unprecedented showcase of government-corporate censorship, to contradict corporate media and "government science," across all mainstream social media platforms, were grounds for account termination. In the early months of 2020, it became heresy to critique covid vaccines and public health government interventions, which included lockdowns and mask mandates. It was also a violation of the terms of service to personally interpret or present covid-19 data in a means contradictory to the mainstream scientific *consensus*. Much of these policies remain intact to this day, over two years later. Let us briefly explore the covid-19 policy of the Google-owned social media platform company known as YouTube.

In a display of Orwellian censorship, YouTube does not to this day allow any information on its platform that "contradicts local health authorities or the World Health Organization's medical information about COVID-19." More specifically, they outlaw "claims about COVID-19 vaccination that contradict expert consensus from local health authorities or the WHO." It also remains a violation to "dispute the efficacy of…WHO's guidance on physical distancing to reduce transmission of COVID-19." The display of information that claims "masks do not play a role in preventing the contraction and transmission of COVID-19" is also prohibited. A giant social media platform that prides itself on providing a digital space for humans to freely interact from around the world, in a manner that cannot be made more conspicuous, made it illegal to critique government decree, or "public health" mandates. It is only a matter of time before these social media platforms outwardly prohibit information that critiques the "efficacy" of vaccine passports. Thankfully, the authority of these companies is limited to the digital world and has no bearing on the free enterprise of literature. The government, and its bedded corporations, have no place on these pages.

Social media platforms paid homage to George Orwell as they designated government health authorities, and the World Health Organization, the gatekeepers to reality, truth, and science. There is incredible irony in censoring debate and information, in the form of conversation, that does not adhere to the "scientific authority." As George Orwell made clear half a century ago, the *Ministry of Truth* and the *Ministry of Peace* are about anything but truth and peace. The same applies today to the Ministry of Science and, especially, to any bureaucrat who labels themselves the "Minister of Science."

With the gift of time, I had the pleasure of witnessing the surreal backtracking of YouTube's censorship policy and the failed attempt of gatekeeping what is considered "misinformation." Leading up to the covid vaccination rollout, and shortly after, all major social media platforms including YouTube prohibited the claim that covid vaccines could lead to blood clots. They labeled it as misinformation and treated such as a conspiracy theory. Any individual, with or without supposed credentials, who made said claim or alluded to it as a possibility was outright suspended and banned. At the time, their reason was that it contradicted local health authorities and the WHO. The "misinformation" might have also *dissuaded* someone from the covid vaccine, and that was an intolerable offense during the war on covid. The policy that prohibited the mention of blood clots as a side-effect to covid vaccines, however, suddenly disappeared. Their reason was that the Centers for Disease and Control (CDC), which is the national public health agency of the United States, and the WHO openly admitted that covid vaccines carried the risk of blood clotting. The same hypocrisy applied to heart inflammation, which was labeled as a side-effect on covid vaccines after it had been similarly dubbed as misinformation.

Social media platforms simulated a totalitarian dystopia, displaying the dangers present in such a reality. As is the case in any totalitarian regime, reality and truth are only reality and truth once the government says it is. For the purpose of drawing another reference to George Orwell's *1984*, two plus two equals four until the Ministry of Education convinces you otherwise. It may very well become five, and any mention of four would be censored and treated as misinformation. If the years between 2020 and 2022 were any indication, the government need only say "the science had changed," or in this analogy, "the math had changed." Therein lies the fundamental issue when government, or any centralized "authority," presumes itself the gatekeeper of information; the gatekeeper to truth; and the gatekeeper to speech. Despite the fallacy demonstrated in the labeling of information as "misinformation," and the problematic nature of censorship, the President of the United States, Joe Biden, pleaded with media platforms to turn even more Orwellian. In a White House press briefing on January 13, 2022, Biden called on corporations to embody completely the will of the State:

> *"I make a special appeal to social media companies and media outlets — please deal with the misinformation and disinformation that's on your shows. It has to stop."*[3]

Kamran Abbasi, editor-in-chief for the British Medical Journal (BMJ) had this to say during a bout of friendly fire with technology conglomerate Meta's (formally Facebook) covid-19 censorship policies:

> *"We should all be very worried that Facebook, a multibillion-dollar company, is effectively censoring fully fact checked journalism that is raising legitimate concerns about the conduct of clinical [vaccine] trials. Facebook's actions won't stop The BMJ doing what is right, but the real question is: why is Facebook acting in this way? What is driving its world view? Is it ideology? Is it commercial interests? Is it incompetence? Users should be worried that, despite presenting itself as a neutral social media platform, Facebook is trying to control how people think under the guise of 'fact checking.'"[4]*

It was, however, not Facebook that was trying to control or regulate how people think. They were merely the hands of those who directed the company to do as such. The puppeteer that directed social media platforms to mobilize against information that discouraged covid vaccination, and disobedience to "public health" mandates, was unsurprisingly the government. The collusion between government and social media platforms to censor divergent narratives surrounding the covid vaccine crusade was further exposed after the CDC's internal communications were made public by *The Washington Free Beacon* on July 27, 2022. The leaked documents confirmed the following:

> *"Over the course of at least six months, starting in December of 2020, CDC officials regularly communicated with personnel on Twitter, Facebook, and Google over 'vaccine misinformation.' At various times CDC officials would flag specific posts by users on social media platforms such as Twitter as 'example posts.'"[5]*

Social media companies that agreed to act on behalf of the government, which ushered in an unprecedented era of digital censorship, notably engaged in market manipulation. Alongside other major digital platforms, YouTube prohibited any "content that recommends use of Ivermectin...or home remedies...for the treatment of COVID-19." Without making any explicit claim as to the reasons governments recruited multinational corporations to pigeonhole treatment discourse for covid-19, the fact that home remedies and ivermectin, among other generic remedies, are non-patented is telling. Generic drugs and any treatment product not patented means that profits are not concentrated into the hands of a few, which is problematic for government and bedded pharmaceutical investors and lobbyists. In general, competition in the market proves problematic for any government subsidized service which is why they so often ban or undermine independent alternatives.

To reiterate, multinational technology companies and social media platforms collaborated with government agencies to undermine the market of social and economic exchange. While they blatantly engaged in propaganda, these companies also participated in what could only be defined as profiteering. To accuse these parties of profitable manipulation is not an accusation in the slightest, but a mere fact of reality. On December 1, 2021, one week following the announcement of the covid-19 variant *omicron*, the eight largest shareholders for Pfizer and Moderna made over a combined ten billion dollars.[6] These shareholders included prominent investing management companies Vanguard Group Inc. and Blackrock Inc., as well as the Government Pension Fund of Norway. Two of *The Big Three* investment management companies, Blackrock and Vanguard, the latter being the largest shareholder of the former, are the top institutional shareholders for Google and their subsidiary, YouTube. The two investment management companies are also large shareholders among a range of other *Big Tech* companies including Meta Inc., which owns Facebook and Instagram.

One might also find it peculiar that the Norwegian government was a primary institutional stakeholder in one of the largest vaccine producers, especially considering they subsidized that same product and distributed it "freely" to its citizens. The Norwegian taxpayer was evidently used to invest and subsidize a company and its production line. This exploitation was the norm for the majority of countries whose governments purchased covid vaccines, with funds taken from the pockets of the ordinary citizen, before mandating it upon them.

Without falling deep into the rabbit hole, technology conglomerates like Google and Meta, and their related branch of shareholders, invested in and profited off the coercive government distribution of covid vaccines. The mantra that "vaccination is the only way forward," repeated extensively by self-proclaimed "world leaders," including Canadian Prime Minister Justin Trudeau, was a slogan profitable to the bureaucratic and corporate elites. This seeming network of governments, large corporations, and State-invested shareholders is not a profound conspiracy. On the contrary, it is in part how corporatism or economic fascism in Canada, America, and the west operates. The quasi-fascist system that has culminated in modern-day democratic societies date back to the popularity of Italy's fascism in the early twentieth century under the leadership of Benito Mussolini. At the time, the west openly applauded Mussolini and wished to replicate the cohesiveness of Italy's economic and social system.

George Soule, a liberal editor for the American magazine *New Republic*, prophetically declared in 1934 that America, and consequently Europe, was "trying out the economics of Fascism without having suffered all its social or political ravages."[7] A notably far left-leaning trusted advisor to American president Franklin D. Roosevelt (FDR), Rexford Tugwell, referred to fascism as the "cleanest, neatnest, most efficiently operating piece of social machinery I've ever seen."[8] Even FDR himself, who served as the American president from 1933 to 1945, was "deeply impressed by what he [Mussolini] has accomplished and by his evidenced honest purpose of restoring Italy."[9]

Mussolini similarly praised the American president, as evidenced in his reviews of Roosevelt's *Looking Forward* and *New Frontiers*, the latter written by Roosevelt's secretary of agriculture, Henry A. Wallace. In his writings, Mussolini reflected positively on the fascist elements of FDR's many reforms and programs that centralized government power. A centralization and government expansion that has become the norm in the twenty-first century. In his review of *Looking* Forward, Mussolini wrote:

"The question is often asked in America and in Europe just how much "Fascism" the American President's program contains...Reminiscent of Fascism is the principle that the state no longer leaves the economy to its own devices, having recognized that the welfare of the economy is identical to the welfare of the people. Without question, the mood accompanying this sea change resembles that of Fascism."[10]

Mussolini's appraisal was more candid in his review of *New Frontiers*:

"The book as a whole is just as "corporativistic" as the individual solutions put forth in it...Wallace's answer to the question of what America wants is as follows: anything but a return to the free market, i.e., anarchistic economy. Where is America headed? This book leaves no doubt that it is on the road to corporatism, the economic system of the current

century."[11]

German historian, Wolfgang Schivelbusch, documents that fascism at the turn of the twentieth century was generally considered a "synonym for state control" and "might be more accurately described as social-democratic planning."[12] The fascism that was praised in the early twentieth century and the one that has manifested in the modern day is thus simply a merger of the public and private sector. In other words, it is an economic and social partnership between governments and businesses. The State does not own the private sector but rather wills it in its image.

I have elucidated this fascistic economic and social system permeating our "democratic and free" society as to provide additional explanation and context to the power wielded by governments during their war on covid and the subservience observed by both ordinary citizens and businesses alike. Ironically to some, the fascist or corporatist underbelly of modern democratic governments was most noticeable in Canada. While government-enforced lockdowns and mandates which forcefully closed businesses and violated private property rights are obvious examples, there was another incident more subtly egregious. To implement vaccine passports, the Canadian federal government promised one billion of taxpayer money to help provinces pay for vaccine passports; withheld money to provinces that did not implement passports; and granted legal immunity to compliant employers. Justin Trudeau explicitly stated that he would "protect businesses that mandate vaccinations from unjustified lawsuits."[13]

The way in which "government say" and "business do" is evidently not a new script by any means. The covid vaccine crusade simply attracted more attention to its existence. The deference to the

State in the political, social, and economic realm has been steadily growing for over a century. The government's amassed centralization was merely more visible and demonstrably brutal, albeit efficient, between 2020-2022. In an interview with *Fox Business*, Dave Smith, Libertarian thinker and host of the podcast *Part of The Problem*, bluntly highlighted the fascistic rhetoric of vaccine passport advocates:

> *"If you believe basic human liberties are predicated on the consumption of a product from a giant pharmaceutical company, you are a fascist...This is not businesses deciding that they don't want customers in; this is the government telling businesses that they have no choice."*[14]

The peddlers of government-enforced vaccine passports barked at the accusation of fascism, admitting their ignorance and lack of self-awareness. They contended with this corporatist definition of fascism and instead defined it as the othering of minorities for a militant and nationalistic cause. Even in their own vague conception of fascism, they refused to admit that the democratic west engaged in identical rhetoric against its own citizens who disobeyed government "public health" decrees. The unvaccinated and anti-mandate groups were blatantly othered in the name of national security and turned into second-class citizens by those who were deluded enough to self-proclaim as "anti-fascists."

To conclude the discussion of government collusion with social media platforms, a global "tech giant" peddled government subsidized covid vaccines and consequently monopolized the market. They accomplished such a feat by ensuring covid vaccines were the only product on the market, in relation to covid-19, that was allowed to be discussed and recommended on their platform. These tech corporations, and their institutional and government funded shareholders stood to make obscene profits by a manipulation that ought to be considered profiteering. Alas, such manipulative collusion was both tolerated and applauded by the masses during the derangement syndrome of *unprecedented times*.

The prized judicial court systems of modern-day democracies, aside from legalizing and enabling the onslaught of government *emergency authorized* mandates and passports, upheld their respective government's covid vaccine crusade by setting dystopian precedent regarding the treatment of the unvaccinated. One such precedent pertained to familial disputes. While this judicial precedent was set globally, it was first spearheaded in Canada. The Canadian province of Ontario was one of the first judicial courts in the west that prohibited unvaccinated citizens from serving on juries.[15] One can therefore expect the kind of treatment the unvaccinated were given by the Canadian courts between 2020-2022. In the following, I briefly mention three notably egregious and disheartening court cases.

In December of 2021, a father in Quebec lost visitation rights to his child because as per the decision of Superior Court Justice Sebastien Vaillancourt, "he [was] not vaccinated and [was] opposed to health [government] measures."[16] The judge also referred to the father as a "conspiracy theorist," which is disconcerting coming from a supposed impartial representative of the law.[17] In October of 2021, Ontario Superior Court Justice Jennifer Mackinnon ruled that an unvaccinated mother be legally disallowed to "provide [her] child with any information…about COVID-19 vaccines [that are] contrary to what is provided by the Canadian, Ontario, and Ottawa public health authorities."[18] As it pertained to vaccinating the child, the judge transferred all decision-making or consent power to the vaccinated father.

Akin to the digital space provided by social media platforms, court rooms provided by the government funded judicial system punished any rhetoric that was in contradiction to the will of the State and their covid vaccination campaign. Alas, while social media companies merely terminated accounts as punishment for disobedience, the judicial system terminated family relationships because a parent either spoke out against the government or committed the grave sin of refusing a pharmaceutical product.

On January 31, 2022, leading Justice Nathalie Godbout of the Court of Queen's Bench ordered that an unvaccinated father in New Brunswick lose visitation rights to see his children. The judge declared that the father's refusal to take the covid vaccine due to his own personal risk assessment carried "little to no weight...when measured against the...medical advice of our public health officials."[19] The fact that government commissioned judicial employees upheld government mandates and deified government employed academics should surprise no one. The government's crusade on covid illuminated, like never before, the cohesive and fascistic hegemony that corrodes our modern society.

Another precedent that judicial courts set on behalf of their government employers related to the deportation of the unvaccinated. In January of 2022, tennis player Novak Djokovic was granted a medical exemption, predicated on already having natural covid antibodies, to play in the tennis tournament known as the Australian Open. However, upon his arrival in Melbourne, Djokovic was detained, and his visa revoked. The Australian government argued in court that having an influential unvaccinated tennis player, who exhibited *anti-vax* ideology, play in the tournament would "encourage other people to disregard or act inconsistently with public health advice and policies in Australia."[20] They argued that "anti-vaccination sentiment" and "civil unrest" would increase because of his presence.[21] In other words, the State argued unacceptable thoughts would creep into the minds of its impressionable subjects.

The Australian federal justice system upheld the will of the State and deported Novak Djokovic at the behest of Australia's immigration minister. In a display of hypocrisy, a vaccinated tennis player by the name of Audrey Rublev tested positive on his arrival in Australia while Mr. Djokovic, an unvaccinated tennis player who not only had natural immunity to covid-19 but tested negative, was deported around the same day. The vaccinated player was allowed to isolate in Australia and participate in the Australian Open while his unvaccinated colleagues had their visas suspended and persons deported. The reason being that their biological contents differed as did their beliefs.

Moving on from top-down institutional contributions, ordinary government employees and officials went beyond in their everyday life to contribute to the covid vaccination campaign. One particular contribution was so admirable that it landed a New York public-school science teacher the prospect of four years in prison. The incident involved a teacher who personally vaccinated, in her own home, one of her seventeen-year-old students.[22] The teacher also had the distorted state of mind to think it was a clever idea to film and publicize the incident. Whether it was a symptom of mass hysteria, undying devotion to the crusade, or the deification of pharmaceutical injections, it was unprecedented. While public or government schools have traditionally spearheaded compulsory vaccination, a teacher has never taken it upon themselves to personally vaccinate a student, let alone in her own home.

Aside from being the masterminds behind the implementation and enforcement of vaccine mandates and passports, government bureaucrats made their individual contributions to the cause through more subversive avenues. One of those avenues was controlling the narrative on covid-19 infections through collaborative and scripted public service announcements. In the United States, two senators and one representative not only tested positive for covid on the same day, but they each released an identical message at the exact same time. Democrat Representative, Jason Crow was "thankful to be fully vaccinated and boosted and experiencing only mild symptoms," and ended his announcement by declaring "the vaccine is safe and effective"; Senator Cory Booker was "grateful to have received two doses of [the] vaccine and, more recently, a booster" and concluded the statement with the impossible-to-prove belief that "without them I would be doing much worse."[23] Last but unfortunately not least, Senator Elizabeth Warren was also "grateful for the protection provided against serious illness that comes from being vaccinated and boosted" and remarked that she was "only experiencing mild symptoms."[24] To note, a booster refers to an additional dose of the covid vaccine outside of the initially required doses.

This script was not an isolated incident nor constrained to currently serving government officials. Former President of the United States, Barack Obama, after testing positive for covid-19 on March 13, 2022, stated that he was "grateful to be vaccinated and boosted" and advocated everyone "to get vaccinated if you haven't already."[25] A top donor for the WHO and a self-ordained health official, Bill Gates, also repeated the script after contracting covid. On May 10, 2022, Gates stated that he was "following the expert's advice by isolating" and was "fortunate to be vaccinated and boosted."[26]

Canadian politicians were provided a script identical to the Americans. Considering the country's relationship, Canada may very well have borrowed the script from the American government. After testing positive for covid on June 13, 2022, following a handfuls of round trips around the world whilst millions of unvaccinated Canadians were prohibited from travelling, Justin Trudeau regurgitated the tired-old messaging:

> *"I've tested positive for COVID-19. I'll be following public health guidelines and isolating. I feel okay, but that's because I got my shots. So, if you haven't, get vaccinated – and if you can, get boosted. Let's protect our healthcare system, each other, and ourselves."*[27]

Dr. Eileen de Villa, Toronto's Medical Officer of Health, expectedly joined Trudeau's choir twenty-four hours after his own public announcement because she too had tested positive for the disease. If you would like to participate in a guessing-game of what Dr. Eileen had to say, you are free to do so. Without further ado, Toronto's Medical Officer had this to say following her positive results:

> *"I'm following public health guidelines [and] resting at home. I feel relatively well and owe that to keeping up to date with my COVID-19 vaccines. If you haven't already, get your next eligible dose to protect you, your loved ones and community."*[28]

Following covid infections in vaccinated public officials the script was clear: make a public statement to promote the covid vaccine and reiterate the protection of the vaccine and the importance of a booster. While pushing the covid vaccine campaign, which was steadfast in vaccinating every single human on earth, governments deflected from any questioning of reality. One obvious question, buried beneath the distraction, was how three senators and other government officials, all double, triple, and quadruple vaccinated while surrounded by primarily vaccinated colleagues in predominately vaccinated spaces, ended up infected with some only hours apart. And what did that say about the legitimacy and necessity of lockdowns, mandates, and especially vaccine passports?

With the arrival of the covid vaccine crusade, behaviour and information became regulated in the name of a greater objective. In other words, *for the greater good*. Dissemination of information that did not explicitly advocate its reader to vaccinate was and continues to be deemed dangerous and a liability to both the State and its vocal propagandists, i.e., the peddlers of vaccine passports. This book itself is likely to be similarly critiqued, considering that while I will never compel anyone to refuse or accept covid vaccination, this book calls into question the ethics, the science, the legality, and the sheer existence of vaccine passports. My intention is also to provide context to the conversation of vaccine passports by illuminating the distorted perceptions that permeate the function and nature of vaccination. What the reader wishes to do with my voice is up to them to decide, as I shall not pretend myself on a moral crusade to engineer population behaviour to fit any blueprint for humanity. I am not a government bureaucrat, after all.

PHARMACEUTICALS AND THE STATE

This book aims to dissect the nature and reality of vaccine passports, however, to critique vaccine passports one must make critique possible of vaccines. If someone is entrenched in a cultish orthodoxy towards vaccines, they are unlikely to entertain a negative assessment of vaccine passports and therein lies the issue. It was notoriously taboo to critique vaccine passports in its inception largely because it has remained universally taboo to question vaccines entirely.

One notable phenomenon that fosters this taboo and subsequent orthodoxy, which underpinned the covid vaccination crusade, is the relationship that exists between government and vaccines or, more specifically, the State and pharmaceutical companies. The alliance between pharmaceuticals and government is a global phenomenon in the west. It is, however, largely concentrated and most influential in North America, particularly in the United States and within Canada to a lesser extent.

The largest pharmaceutical companies, often referred to as *"Big Pharma,"* uniquely function as both big business in the economic landscape as well as the intellectual or "expert" authority in the realm of public and social policy. The triangular, hegemonic alliance between government, big business, and the academic central planners of society, who collaborated to normalize vaccine passports, will be expounded later. In this section, I briefly illuminate the ways pharmaceutical companies benefit from their alliance with governments.

Pharmaceutical companies attain some of the following advantages from their alliance with the State: billions of taxpayer dollars for the creation and marketing of their drug products[29], research and development tax credits[30], marketing and advertising tax deductions[31], and maintaining their respective monopolies through patents.[32] The economic and social benefits that culminate from their alliance provide pharmaceutical companies, particularly in the United States, a unique form of legal immunity that rivals the highly regulated and monopolized agricultural industry.

Between the years 2003 and 2016, pharmaceutical company GlaxoSmithKline received twenty-seven penalties and paid close to ten billion in fines; the highest tally among drug companies sampled in one notable study.[33] Pfizer Inc., the pharmaceutical makers behind one of the mRNA covid vaccines, were second on the study's list with eighteen penalties and three billion in fines.[34] Johnson & Johnson, another covid vaccine manufacturer, was third on the list with fifteen penalties and 2.7 billion worth of fines.[35] Out of the twenty-six pharmaceutical companies sampled in the study, thirty-three billion in fines were paid out with the top eleven companies accounting for twenty-eight billion.[36] While these may seem like considerable penalties, they do not make a financial dent on the biggest pharmaceutical companies. This invulnerability is largely due to pharmaceutical companies being given the power to levy government relations and legally plunder the taxpayer through various subsidies. As a result of this partnership, *Big Pharma* simply get their money back and more.

What pharmaceutical companies are prosecuted for also pales in comparison to the immunity they are consistently granted. Governments in the west, particularly the United States, have throughout history bestowed impenetrable immunity to pharmaceutical companies who developed one specific thing: vaccines. Vaccine manufacturers have their legal immunity revoked if they are deemed to have acted in wilful criminal misconduct. Alas, no governmental body in the last century, at least in North America, has recognized such misconduct in relation to vaccines. And it would be naïve to assume that this remains the case because no deception or misconduct has taken place.

Big Pharma's alliance with the State has enabled their sweeping financial domination and subsequent influence and monopoly over political, economic, and social affairs. Given their desire to maintain their position and influence within the higher echelons of society, pharmaceutical companies spend obscene amounts to lobby government officials. Between 1999 and 2018, the largest pharmaceutical companies spent a total of 4.7 billion in federal government lobbying fees, influencing policy and legislation domestically and abroad. [37] This influence, power, and wealth is quite peculiar for what many perceive to be a mere humble, healthcare provider. While pharmaceutical companies generate obscene wealth annually, the government-favoured pharmaceuticals that took part in the covid vaccine crusade made a fortune. In 2021, Pfizer totaled eighty one billion in revenue, which was double what it made in revenue the previous year.[38] Pfizer's covid vaccines in 2021 brought in forty-two billion in revenue, which single-handedly exceeded the company's entire revenue stream the year prior, which totaled forty-one billion.[39] In the first quarter of 2022, Pfizer raked in over thirteen billion "in direct sales and alliance revenues, driven by global uptake including pediatric and [covid] booster doses, following a growing number of regulatory approvals and temporary authorization."[40]

Pfizer's mRNA covid vaccine remains the primary distributer in North America and was the first authorized vaccine in the U.S. for ages under eighteen. Considering what we know of pharmaceuticals, particularly Pfizer Inc., their financial success and preferential treatment regarding the covid vaccine campaign was entirely predictable considering it was deliberately orchestrated. The collusion between Pfizer and other corporate-government interests during the covid vaccine campaign is revisited later in the book. While not an uncommon practice in the pharmaceutical industry, most if not all covid vaccines were primarily subsidized in both development and

31

distribution. This means taxpayers forcefully paid into its creation and delivery. One notable example is the pharmaceutical company Moderna Inc., who received nearly one billion dollars from the United States federal government for covid vaccine development before receiving an additional 1.5 billion supply order in 2020.[41] The quantity of covid vaccines that were purchased between 2020-2022 by governments around the world totaled amounts that some would say could *end* world hunger.

Instead of pharmaceutical companies claiming they had vaccine doses for sale, just like bakers would declare they have loaves for sale, governments announced they themselves had covid vaccines to hand out. It would not have been a vaccine crusade, after all, if governments did not unilaterally mobilize and spearhead its creation and distribution. If the covid vaccine was a voluntary product to be purchased on the market, there would have largely been no issue at all. However, if that were the case billions would not have funneled into the pockets of government officials and pharmaceutical executives. The free market did not exist in the realm of covid vaccines which meant that *freedom* and *choice* were already absent from the equation before the arrival of vaccine passports. The passports and related mandates worked only to bury the free market entirely and freedom along with it.

One subtle sociological phenomenon relevant to the issue of government subsidy, and which contributed to the "efficacy" of the covid vaccination campaign, was the fact that subsidizing "free" covid vaccines compelled people to vaccinate because they already paid for it. Think of it like someone begrudgingly drinking a coffee instead of a tea because the employee got the order wrong. The rationale to drink the coffee is simple: the individual may as well consume the product because they already paid for it. While it is true that you could get a refund from an ordinary business, the same could not have been said for receiving a refund from the government's stockpile of covid vaccines. Individuals who remained unvaccinated also not only paid for a product they refused to consume but were punished for their refusal. This was one of the most criminal aspects of the government's war on covid.

If you would object to a robber offering vaccines with money they directly stole from your pocket, then you ought to object to government officials doing the very same thing. This economic and moral violation would not be tolerated if it were any other product. For example, if governments purchased stockpiles of Tylenol and forced its consumption upon the people. Even for something as "lifesaving" as bread, which was the label prefaced for covid vaccines, people would be opposed if the State purchased stockpiles of them from bakeries and handed them out in designated breadlines. However, people do not perceive vaccines as products to voluntary consume and therefore have no issue with government-subsidized vaccine lines.

IMMUNITY TO CRITICISM

The extent that vaccines provide immunity against disease pales in comparison to the intellectual immunity given to vaccines by government institutions. While the former may be up for academic debate, the latter is not. An individual cannot critique any vaccine let alone openly refuse it without being debased and ridiculed. This immunity to criticism is overtly observed by the Orwellian labels of "antivax" and "vaccine-hesitant," which are labels that have been re-peated into oblivion and not in good faith.

These weaponizing labels first originated in academia and are traditionally used in research, with an abundance of funding going to studies dedicated to identifying and minimizing *anti-vax* and *vaccine-hesitant* sentiment. The former is branded against anyone who critiques or declines a vaccine and or is opposed to compulsory vaccination. The latter term is branded upon anyone who is critical of a vaccine but makes clear their *uncertainty* and inevitable compliance. When translated towards any other product, these two terms seem rather preposterous. Marijuana distributers may as well call skeptics of their product "marijuana-hesitant," with the underlying assumption being that everyone should inevitably use marijuana. Those who are steadfast never to try weed, for medical or recreational purposes, might as well be labeled "anti-marijuana." Someone who does not generally use antibiotics ought to also, ironically, be "anti-antibiotics" or "antibiotic-hesitant" if they use said product but are weary of some of its side-effects. The above examples are transparently absurd as no company, except for vaccine distributers, would dare shame and harass its consumer for not using its products.

To indulge in any critique of vaccines is to be placed in one of two boxes, with both labels inherently implying that critique is innately misguided. The "antivax" are perceived as malevolent souls that ought to be ostracized in the name of *saving lives* while the "vaccine-hesitant" are the victims of propaganda that need *guidance* into the light. One label is designated for the villain, the other the victim. The content of the critique is irrelevant; what matters is what label they represent and what extent they are to be ostracized, censored, and re-educated. Avoiding the ominous label of "anti-vax," people with unconventional critiques voluntarily place themselves in the "hesitant" box. They willingly distort, weaken, and discredit their own viewpoint in fear of being labeled. One notable example is the case of Gananoque, Ontario town councillor Mike Kench, who after being suspended for critiquing vaccine passports, responded by stating on the record, in an interview with *Global News*, that he did not describe himself as anti-vax but rather "vaccine hesitant."[42] Given the irrelevancy of such a scripted confession, Mr. Kench's clarifying statement was likely prompted by a media reporter who wanted to give the councillor an opportunity to clear his name and *set the record straight*.

The hostile climate surrounding vaccine criticism leads many to claim they are not "anti-vax" whenever expressing their critiques towards vaccines and or compulsory immunization. It is as if they are swearing under oath and ready to be the subject of a trial – and to be fair, they truly are on trial. Anyone who dares make known their unconventional views towards vaccines risks being smeared publicly, terminated from their employment, and outright suspended from whatever platform from which they had spoken. If social media functioned the same way in real life, anyone accused of being "anti-vax" would be *deleted* from the public.

This vilification was observed among prominent actors who voiced their critiques of the covid vaccines or admitted they were unvaccinated. While censoring actors for unconventional vaccine views has never been uncommon, the severity intensified between 2020-2022. During the covid vaccine crusade, any actor that was accused of being anti-vax was subjected to a witch-hunt and became victim to boycotts and petitions demanding their employment termination. Two publicized victims of the covid vaccine witch-trials were actresses Gina Carano and Letitia Wright.

Carano was one of the first in the film industry to openly speak out against the "public health" mandates, lockdowns, and vaccine passports. She was blunt in both her critique of covid vaccine mandates and the notion that basic liberties are gatekept behind a pharmaceutical product. Alas, she was debased and branded as anti-mask, anti-lockdown, and anti-vax. She was accused of undermining the efficacy and importance of the covid vaccine campaign, and that was enough of a reason to have her career guillotined. Humorously, she was even branded as pro-virus because apparently if you opposed government mandates combatting a germ, you were pro-germ.

You can predict how this story ended. Following her vocal critiques, Gina was terminated from her employment in Disney's TV series, *The Mandalorian* and blacklisted from Hollywood. Along the same lines that this very book is likely to be critiqued, Gina Carano was accused of sharing views that *discouraged* people from getting vaccinated. When it came to the covid vaccine crusade, remarks that conflicted with the mission of the board, written by government and pharmaceutical bureaucrats, were aggressively censored. In parallel to Gina Carano, *Newsweek* reported the following on November 11, 2021, pertaining to actress Letitia Wright:

> *"Black Panther fans are demanding that Letitia Wright be removed as the lead actor in the hit Marvel movie's sequel, if claims she has refused to take the covid vaccine turn out to be true."*[43]

Media articles that reported on Letitia Wright prefaced her name with "Alleged Anti-Vaxxer,"[44] as if the label were to indicate a criminal offense not yet proven in a court of law. While on the subject of criminal charges, actors critical of the covid vaccines arguably received more financial and social backlash than actors accused of sexual misconduct. Or at the very least, critiquing the vaccines garnered just as much backlash which was troubling either way.

This immunity to criticism as a general phenomenon hangs over all sectors of society, as though to speak ill of vaccines is to utter the name of Harry Potter's archnemesis *Voldemort*; a fictional villain in J.K. Rowling's novel series. Anyone brazen enough to articulate any critique of vaccines is accompanied by a crowd filled with silence and panic, as if everyone is expecting the arrival of "he who must not be named." This taboo did not organically come to fruition. No child naturally grows up fearing ostracization for refusing a pharmaceutical product, nor are they inclined to judge or fear their *unvaccinated* counterparts. The labeling surrounding vaccine discourse is deliberate, unique, and reared its ugliest of heads with the covid vaccines.

No product other than vaccines has more safeguards to ensure conformity and immunity from criticism. This immunity was perfectly and humorously capsulated by the case of Brazilian president, Jair Bolsonaro. The president was suspended off social media, in October of 2021, and had an investigation opened against him by the Brazilian Supreme Court.[45] The reason was that the president shared an opinion that covid vaccines might raise the likelihood of developing an acquired immunodeficiency syndrome (AIDS). Such a drastic response would have anyone first presume treason were involved or some action that compromised national security. Alas, it took only an unconventional vaccine opinion for the government and its courts to mobilize such an attack on their own president. In the global covid vaccination crusade that enveloped the world, critiquing covid vaccines had in fact become an act of treason and a threat to *national security.*

The relationship between vaccines and freedom passports, and the unprecedented devotion witnessed towards covid vaccine passports, was predicated on three deliberately cultivated psychological and sociological factors that politicized and distorted vaccine perception. To elaborate, these psychosocial factors have distorted vaccine discourse to the point where vaccines are viewed as gifts from the divine. Before these factors are discussed in the following chapter, it is interesting to note how this unnatural distinction, which separates vaccines from pharmaceutical products, explains why many liberals, once known to be critical of big pharmaceuticals and their history of corruption and profiteering, paradoxically became the crusaders of covid vaccines and defenders of pharmaceutical corporations. When once the left was critical of pharmaceuticals and their lobbying power, they are to be remembered following the year 2020 as the group that adhered religiously to pharmaceutical executives and followed blindly all government "health" mandates that forced pharmaceutical injections onto the individual. If conservatives are to be stereotyped as the "party of big business," then modern liberals ought to hence be referred to as the "party of big pharmaceuticals" and the "party of government mandates." With that said, both conservative and liberal governments – exposing further their façade – implemented vaccine passports and other dystopian covid mandates.

Chapter 4

BUILDING BLOCKS TO

VACCINE UNIFORMITY

The subject which will be of most importance politically is mass psychology...Its importance has been enormously increased by the growth of modern methods of propaganda. Of these the most influential is what is called "education" ...[I]n time anybody will be able to persuade anybody of anything if he can catch the patient young and is provided by the State with money and equipment. This subject will make great strides when it is taken up by scientists under a scientific dictatorship.

Bertrand Russell[1]

The unwavering dogma surrounding vaccine passports between 2020-2022 stemmed from a complexity of factors. While aspects of the covid vaccine crusade have since been highlighted, it is another thing entirely to understand why, and how, such authoritarianism became so beloved and accepted. Prior to the year 2020, no one would have expected the masses to flock cheerfully to the idea of showing proof of medical injections to enter café's, theatres, gyms, and trains. The question therefore is what primed the population to adopt the notion of vaccine passports so suddenly. While obsessive news coverage that made spectacle of every covid-19 death contributed to the support for vaccine passports, more subtle yet pervasive contributions predated 2020.

Three *building blocks* have contributed to vaccine uniformity and consequently to the dogmatic acceptance and advocacy of covid vaccine mandates and passports. These notable building blocks, or psychosocial factors, include the utopian recollection of vaccines, the conformity of vaccine perception to the dominant collectivist ideology, and the savior complex that permeates vaccine culture.

A MYTHICAL HISTORY

To understand how covid vaccinations became a collectivist symbol with an impenetrable immunity to criticism, we ought to first address the utopian, mythical recollection of vaccination that permeate modern society. These utopian distortions have led to the view of vaccines as a holy grail and catalyst for human existence, which stands in contrast to what they physically are – a pharmaceutical product. Vaccines are a product created by a pharmaceutical company and in that sense, they are no different to aspirin, Tylenol, and cough medicine. This fact highlights the troubles of enforcing vaccines through legislation and policy, as well as subsidizing them to the masses.

With that said, vaccines are more invasive than typical pharmaceutical products, considering the fact that they function to make an irreversible addition, or change, to the contents of an immune system and require a needle-injection administered by a medical professional. This change is seemingly starker in the mRNA vaccines, which likely contributed to the heightened resistance towards compulsory covid vaccination. Thus, vaccines are simply an invasive medical intervention but alas, when compared to other pharmaceutical interventions, questioning, critiquing, or declining a vaccine follows unprecedented backlash and hostility. Individuals generally respect another's choice to use the *medicine* of their own choosing, predicated upon everyone's unique predilections and bodily needs and desires. This tolerance, however, does not extend to vaccinations; a double standard rooted in the perception of vaccines as products of divinity. It is this deification that cultivates a collectivist and cultist orientation surrounding vaccine usage. To understand the collectivism that permeates vaccine culture, we must first expose the extent to which vaccines are held atop a pedestal.

The obsessive devotion to vaccines stem from the belief that vaccinations are the holy grail of humanity: the divine chalice that eradicated diseases decimating humanity and made possible the drastic increase of the human population and life expectancy. Followers of this romanticized history attribute vaccinations to their human existence and for the world they were born into. One might find it easy to substitute "vaccines" with "God" in the verses recited at grace and find no difference at all. For the holders of these beliefs, their hostility and defensiveness to any criticism of such a divine gift is understandable. Akin to the religious person who may hold disbelief to a person *misguided* enough to reject the significance or teachings of their god or prophet, one may also find someone presenting similar disbelief to anyone who dares *reject* a vaccine. The comparison of vaccine and religious fanaticism and conversion is revisited at the end of the chapter.

The commonly held historical retellings of vaccines are both inaccurate and deceptively simplified. The most generic of these myths is the distorted belief that vaccines *eradicated* an array of viruses plaguing humanity throughout the nineteen and twentieth century. Before the misleading nature of this belief is discussed, it is imperative to mention the injuries and deaths ensued universally by vaccine complications. Prominent examples of complications following mass-vaccination include the swine flu vaccine of 1976, which was associated with increased reports of Guillain-Barre Syndrome, and the oral poliovirus vaccine which infamously caused paralysis, referred to as vaccine-associated paralytic poliomyelitis. Vaccines have also led to the creation of virus strains, including vaccine-derived polio. In fact, the *Associated Press* reported in 2019 that there were "now more children being paralyzed by viruses originating in vaccines than in the wild."[2] Given the existence of vaccine-complications alone, it ought to be an immoral injustice to have such a product coerced onto another person.

The distorted perception towards vaccines does not spare even the most supposedly objective and honest scientists. This perversion was notably observed by a group of researchers involved in one prominent vaccine study of chickens. The study to be hereto discussed also humbles the zealous view of vaccines by offering insights into the dangers of *leaky* vaccines. The following study therefore does not only illustrate the distorted matrix permeating vaccines, but it emphasizes the importance of having vaccines be made optional and voluntary.

The study concluded that "vaccines that do not prevent transmission can create conditions that promote the emergence of pathogen strains that cause more severe disease in unvaccinated hosts."[3] Despite this troubling finding, the researchers echoed sentiments that encouraged vaccinating humans akin to domesticated chickens. In the study, published in 2015, researchers found that the vaccine used by the poultry industry to combat Marek disease had contributed to an evolution of more virulent strains that placed unvaccinated chickens at risk. The researchers noted that the Marek disease virus was drastically deadlier in 2015 than it was in the 1950's; however, they noted that the issue has caused minor problems because every chicken in the industry gets vaccinated anyway.

They also examined this phenomenon in avian influenza; a phenomenon referred to as the *imperfect vaccine hypothesis*. The theory posits that "vaccines that keep hosts alive but still allow transmission could thus allow very virulent strains to circulate in a population."[4] In the study, researchers found that "the most-virulent strain of avian influenza now decimating poultry flocks worldwide can kill unvaccinated birds in just under three days."[5] The researchers further noted that "in the United States and Europe, the birds that get avian influenza are culled, so no further evolution of the virus is possible... [while] farmers in Southeast Asia use vaccines that leak – so the evolution of the avian influenza virus toward greater virulence can happen."[6]

The study demonstrated that "the use of leaky vaccines can promote the evolution of nastier 'hot' viral strains that put unvaccinated individuals at greater risk"[7]. Alas, the concluding remarks by the researchers exemplify the dehumanizing and distorted perception towards vaccine usage in humans. The authors of the study concluded that their findings actually "provide strong evidence for the importance of getting vaccinated" because "when more-virulent strains takes place as a result of vaccination practices, it is the unvaccinated who are at the greater risk."[8] One of the lead researchers of the study, Andrew Read, reaffirmed the study's conclusions, stating that "if you vaccinate all the individuals in a population against a virus, it does not matter if the virus has become super virulent so long as the vaccine continues to be effective."[9]

The pharmaceutical-vaccine industrial complex seems content to undermine medical consent and treat humans as disposable so long as they can market, subsidize, and mandate their products. The fact that this risk posed by vaccination is treated in academia as justification for compulsory and subsidized vaccination policies, to protect the human population from more deadly vaccine-induced strains, exemplifies how distorted perceptions have become. To an individual who does not equate humans to poultry livestock, this scientific finding would incentivize the contrary. The response would rationally be to reduce the use of leaky vaccines as to limit the evolution of more virulent strains in order to both protect the organic biological makeup of humans and avoid creating an environment where vaccine-consent indirectly ceases to exist.

The idea that it would be better to achieve mass conformity towards a medical procedure, i.e., forcing a population to accept a pharmaceutical injection, as the only means for individuals to survive and live is simply villainous. The conclusions made by the authors of this study are representative of the mainstream view towards immunization, and the silence towards these dystopian remarks further highlights the matrix that has permeated vaccination. This matrix may be best described as the docility of a society indoctrinated into the belief that it ought to accept blindly whichever vaccination is administered to them. "It is just a vaccine," after all.

I have briefly dedicated time to illustrate vaccine complications as to highlight the known and unknown side effects, both minor and fatal, that permeate vaccines universally. All medical interventions involve the possibility of risk; hence they unilaterally require some form of consent. Mentioning the reality of risk is not to undermine the value present in a vaccine but merely to reiterate that no matter its apparent significance, consent and the acknowledgement of its risk has always been rightfully required for its use. The recognition of such risks is also why it is paramount to be given the freedom and capacity to refuse vaccination, regardless of the personal reasons involved. This risk acknowledgment is also of utmost relevance when discerning the grave injustice of covid vaccine passports. While heart inflammation and blood clots were a widely acknowledged side effect of the most prominent covid vaccines, after being initially disputed, such an admission did little to dissuade passport and mandate supporters. Even to this day, as some passports have *temporarily* rescinded, there are fervent advocates who wish for it back.

The fundamental issue of medical risk as it pertained to covid vaccines was notably highlighted by a United States Food and Drug Administration (FDA) court-ordered document. The court document made public Pfizer's clinical trial data that was used to grant emergency authorization for its distribution. The document report, submitted by Pfizer-BioNTech as part of its Biological License Application to the FDA, was released to the public in the beginning of 2022. The document, titled *Cumulative Analysis of Post-authorization Adverse Events Reports*, featured an appendix that outlined hundreds of observed adverse events following Pfizer's covid vaccination. These events included, but were not limited to, cardiac failure, brain stem thrombosis, acute kidney injury, and deep vein thrombosis (blood clotting).[10] While the observation of adverse events does not indicate causation, they do indicate, at the very least, a possible correlation. The court-ordered document helps cement the basic and undisputable fact that all vaccines accompany risk, whether *scientifically observed* or not, and thus should never be made mandatory. We ought to never compel anyone to participate in Russian roulette even if the bullet-to-chamber ratio is in the decimals and its safety has been deemed *statistically significant*.

The court-released Pfizer documents also revealed a dark reality in the broader covid vaccination crusade. The FDA was in fact aware, from the beginning, that blood clotting and heart-related complications were a probable adverse effect associated with the covid vaccines. Despite their foresight, governmental health agencies around the world, including the FDA, Health Canada, and European Medicines Agency, only placed labels of "rare heart risk" to the mRNA covid vaccines in the summer of 2021. Health agencies responsible for authorizing covid vaccine distribution and subsequent mandates evidently warned the populace of a "possibility," which they had already suspected, months into their national and global rollout. Governments and vaccine distributors were seemingly aware of the possible adverse reactions from the very beginning. Alas, that did not dissuade them from waiting months until human lives were ruined before placing warning labels. It also did not stop them from censoring anyone who initially purported the possible risk of heart-related complications from the vaccine. And most egregious of all, the risks and labels did nothing to deter governments from implementing sweeping vaccine mandates and passports that compelled millions to take the covid vaccine or have their life upended.

The simplified and glorified belief that pharmaceutical companies heroically came to the rescue, with miracle injections, to save humanity refrains from crediting a far more significant contribution – the economic developments and subsequent technological and infrastructural advancements in hygiene and sanitation. It was these improvements that contributed significantly to the lessening exposure, severity, and subsequent "eradication" of many harmful germs and diseases – including those often solely credited to vaccination. The nineteenth century urbanization boom, which resulted from unprecedented migration into the cities, initially led to chronic overcrowding, impoverished housing, and a lack of infrastructure for clean water and water-disposal systems. As a consequence, the initial stages of industrialization brought a plethora of frequent disease outbreaks including, but not limited to, cholera, dysentery, tuberculosis, typhoid, influenza, and yellow fever. The early twentieth century, on the other hand, brought forth unprecedented advancements to infrastructure and subsequent living conditions, including clean water and functioning sewage disposal systems. These improvements drastically reduced the occurrence and fatality of diseases which plagued predominately urban regions. It can hence be said that these diseases were largely "man-made," or in other words exacerbated by human behaviour.

Vaccines have a record of arriving late to the party while attempting to take all the credit, and there are two notable examples of this phenomena. In North America and much of the west, childhood immunization regiments include vaccines for diphtheria and pertussis (or whooping cough). The commonly held belief is that these vaccines eradicated both diseases that scourged the populace throughout the nineteen and twentieth century. This mythical story, however, is both deceptive and misleading. Jason Waterman's 1927 report, titled *Diphtheria in the United States*, elucidates a reality of diphtheria that runs contrary to what is purported by vaccine makers and government health agencies. In the first year that Bureau of the Census began reporting diphtheria death rates in the death registration area of the United States, in the year 1900, they documented 43.3 deaths per one-hundred thousand in the population.[11] In 1925,

47

Waterman observed that the Census had reported 7.8 deaths per one-hundred thousand.[12] He further noted a similar decrease documented by the Metropolitan Life Insurance Company, which covered parts of Canada and the United States. The insurance company recorded 27.3 deaths per one-hundred thousand in 1911 and 9.5 deaths per one hundred thousand in 1926.[13] The diphtheria vaccine was developed in the early 1920's in America, and introduced in Canada in 1926, however was only widely distributed in both countries in the 1930s.

Such a drastic decrease in diphtheria mortality, which indicates reduced circulation, reported in the United States and Canada in the early twentieth century, could not be possibly explained by the vaccine. The incidence and severity of diphtheria continued its trend, following vaccine distribution, and declined throughout the remaining century. Unsurprisingly, credit for its reduction has been placed solely upon the miracle of vaccine makers and government immunization protocols. The decline of diphtheria mortality during the twentieth century was similarly observed with pertussis, or whooping cough, as displayed by Epidemiologist C.C. Dauer in his 1943 paper, *Reported Whooping Cough Morbidity and Mortality in the United States*. In a similar analysis of the Registration States conducted by Jason Waterman towards diphtheria, Dauer observed the following:

> *"[D]uring the 5-year period from 1900 the mortality was 10.2 per one hundred thousand…[and] beginning about 1925 mortality from whooping cough began to decline rapidly so that the rate for the 5-year period from 1935 to 1939 was only 1.8, a decline of about 80 percent in 15 years."*[14]

The pertussis vaccine was only introduced in the United States around the 1940s, and therefore could not once again explain such a drastic decline. Akin to the trends that accompanied a host of other diseases which historically inflicted over-crowded urban populations, incidence and mortality rates of whooping cough continued to decline throughout the twentieth century. Alas, the pertussis vaccine has also been given credence to such a supposed achievement, chalking up a decrease in a disease's occurrence and severity to the pharmaceutical industry once more. This commonly held belief persists despite the fact that whooping cough has yet to even be eradicated and is, ironically, steadily increasing in the United States today.

The connection between infrastructure and living conditions towards the overall reduction of harmful diseases was further espoused by two researchers in England: Jamie Bartram, a professor at the University of Leeds, and Sandy Cairncross, an epidemiologist at the London School of Hygiene and Tropical Medicine. In their study, they demonstrated that a "massive disease burden" is linked with improper hygiene, sanitation, and water supply.[15] The two researchers ultimately concluded that hygiene, sanitation, and water were the "forgotten foundations of health."[16] I wonder the culprit responsible for this forgetfulness in our modern day.

The litany of reasons which contributed to the decrease of both disease occurrence and severity throughout the twentieth century has ceased to matter in public discourse. If the reason does not start with the letter "V," its significance has been neglected and minimized. The populace has comfortably rested on the cookie-cutter and spoon-fed belief that all these diseases were slain with one fell swoop by the miracles of pharmaceuticals coming to the defense of a frail and dying species.

The contributions of vaccines on the increase in human population and life expectancy is similarly minute compared to the general theme of economic advancements. More specifically, the advancements in infrastructure, manufacturing, production, and notably agriculture which all made possible the sustaining and maintaining of an expansive population. After all, even if you found the cure-all-vaccine for every ailment on earth, the human population would remain indefinitely small without mass-production, i.e., industrialization.

The global population at the turn of the Industrial Revolution experienced an upward trend prior to the uniform distribution of vaccinations. This increase accelerated in the late eighteen and nineteenth century. The populations in major European countries notably doubled in size in the early eighteen century primarily as a result of agricultural production of potatoes, among other reformed food crops. This increase officially boomed in the twentieth century, as infrastructural and manufacturing ingenuity enabled a growing population by making accessible the resources required for a sustainable life. Alas it seems that for population growth and life expectancy, vaccinations arrived late to the party once again but have nonetheless taken credit.

A notable factor that relates to the increase in life expectancy is the decline of infant and child mortality. A significant contribution to the decline in infant mortality has been the technological ingenuity in childbirth and infant care. These improvements have led to the reduction of fatal pregnancy complications as well as enhanced survivability of infants born premature or with severe birth defects. Researchers Bartram and Cairncross also emphasized, in their study, that the "one disease alone [killing] more young children each year than HIV/AIDs, tuberculosis, and malaria combined…is diarrhoea."[17] The leading contributions to reducing the occurrence, severity, and fatality of diarrhoea and related diseases, as espoused by the researchers, is "hygiene, sanitation, and water."[18] As mentioned prior, these three contributors are products of economic and infrastructural ingenuity; not pharmaceutical drugs.

The belief that vaccines led to the miraculous gift of extended life stems, in part, from a misguided notion that the human body is, in its natural state, fragile and disease stricken. Such a pessimistic view of humanity has been infamously influenced by the Hobbesian belief that life, in its natural state, is *nasty, brutish, and short*. While modern advancements in technology, infrastructure, and agriculture rekindled the life expectancy of individuals once subjected to crowded, sedentary, and unsanitary settlements, evidence pertaining to hunter-gathering societies further break the Hobbesian myth. Hunter-gathering and nomadic societies, contrary to popular belief, have maintained life expectancy averages not so dissimilar to those living today in "developed" countries. One such example comes from the indigenous forager peoples of lowland Bolivia, the Tsimané, who have a reported lifespan of seventy years.[19] While this may come as surprise, it is consistent with the notion that homo sapiens have a "characteristic life span," with human bodies functioning "well for about seven decades."[20]

A critic can argue the extent that vaccines contribute to the decrease in infant mortality in the modern day. However, vaccines cannot possibly be the reason hunter-gathering societies have survived to ages parallel to their modern settler-counterparts. This observation, among others, leads to one overarching and relevant conclusion: the human body does not owe its life to vaccines, let alone any pharmaceutical injection or drug of the sort. My goal is not to specifically dismiss vaccines, for they do carry value to the extent that they are treated as pharmaceutical products to be voluntarily purchased and administered. That is, like any other medicinal, medical, or health product on the market. If no one is to be compelled and coerced into buying medicinal products or undergoing medical procedures, then no one should be coerced to purchase and or be administered a vaccine.

This basic consistency would normally exist if pharmaceutical companies were not incentivized, through government immunity and subsidies, to aggressively market their products onto individuals and in some cases have their products outright mandated to consume. To reiterate, my intentions have been twofold. First, to humble over-zealous rhetoric espoused by vaccine passport crusaders fervent in their desire to implant a guilty conscience upon anyone who wishes for bodily autonomy. My second intention has been to illuminate the distorted history of vaccine significance so as to demonstrate both its contributions to the fanatical devotion towards covid vaccines and the uniform acceptance, and advocacy, of vaccine passports.

THE COLLECTIVIST GRAIL

The philanthropic and communal view of vaccination – that it is the savior of humanity and the gift that enabled the prosperity of man – has made it the perfect candidate to embody fundamental collectivist predilections. By acknowledging this symbiotic relationship, between vaccines and collectivism, it becomes easier to both understand why covid vaccines were given to the State, to hand out with an iron fist, and why being vaccinated was considered a pledge of allegiance.

The covid vaccine crusade was accompanied by some absurd, and eerie, collectivist mantras. To medically inject yourself became the ultimate embodiment of "doing your part" for the world, society, and community. Getting the covid vaccine solely for yourself, as a personal medical decision, was a narrative long abandoned. Its crusaders would not have dared be so *selfish* and *individualistic*. The most devote of covid vaccine advocates even conceded they were not worried about contracting covid-19 but instead vaccinated for a litany of altruistic reasons. They vaccinated "for their grandparents," "for their community," "for humanity," and the most philanthropic of them all: "for others."

While one may truly be heart-warmed by these slogans, anyone familiar with groupthink understands that dissent is met with hostility and tyranny. In the echo chamber of the collectivist campaign to "do your part," "we are in this together," and "vaccinate for others," anyone who stood in opposition was ignored, ostracized, and outright ridiculed. This same hostility is generally observed in times of war towards anyone who disagrees with the war effort and declines to praise the troops. They are branded pacificists and isolationists. In this case, instead of a failure to support the troops, it was a failure to praise the covid vaccine and support the dictate of public health troops, i.e., government officials and pharmaceutical bureaucrats.

As a habit of socialists and the newly collectivist-minded peddlers of vaccine passports, who remain a vibrant faction to this day, resistance on the premise of liberty is nefariously mischaracterized. Anyone who refused the covid vaccine or its vaccine passport was labeled as being against vaccines entirely and as antagonistic towards the notion of *togetherness* and community. In advocating for anything to be voluntary, optional, or by choice, and for communal-orientated actions to not be predicated upon coercion or blind conformity, they labeled you the antithesis to community and altruism altogether. One of the most prominent and influential nineteenth century classical liberalists and economists, Claude-Frédéric Bastiat, exposed prophetically this dichotomous fallacy common in collectivist ideologies:

> *"Socialism, like the ancient ideas from which it springs, confuses the distinction between government and society. As a result of this, every time we object to a thing being done by government, the socialists conclude that we object to its being done at all...We disapprove of state education. Then the socialists say that we are opposed to any education. We object to a state religion. Then the socialists say that we want no religion at all...It is as if the socialists were to accuse us of not wanting persons to eat because we do not want the state to raise grain."*[21]

These collectivist contradictions prophetically manifested among advocates of vaccine passports, as will be made abundantly apparent throughout this book. A divine devotion to vaccines, accompanied by a politically relevant collectivist ideology, evidently cultivated the cultish defense of covid vaccinations and vaccine passports. In defining and highlighting the *vaccine matrix*, my intent is to make the criticism of vaccine passports more comprehensible and palpable. There are some perspectives that are so censored from public discourse that individuals are prone to reject them reactively. A seed of doubt and curiosity need to first be planted; a seed that has hopefully been kindled thus far.

SAVIOR COMPLEX

The third psychosocial factor or building block, which contributes to the coercive campaign towards vaccine uniformity, is the savior-complex phenomena. In the context of vaccines, this phenomenon is best described as a self-righteous desire to "save" another person through the assistance of something only that individual can uniquely provide, which would be their particular vaccine. One way to illuminate this phenomenon is to observe its similarities to other forms of savior complexes commonly manifested under the umbrella of imperialism. The savior complex permeating vaccine culture can be more appropriately referred to as pharmaceutical imperialism, which is the fanatical and philanthropic desire to spread around the world a *life-saving* drug.

The deification of vaccines naturally makes it the most popular pharmaceutical product or drug to embody the imperialist complex. After all, vaccines are not only labeled as "life-saving," but they are outright mandated in other countries *for people's own good*. As a consequence, vaccines are also one of the only pharmaceutical products that pickpocket consumers by having their production and distribution entirely subsidized by governments. Vaccines are considered too important to be left to the free market and instead governments are obliged, in their "social contract," to provide them to their citizenry. Such a product is a gift from the divine, and the individual would therefore have to be demented to *reject* such an offering.

Aside from the glaring financial incentives, the fanatical desire to spread vaccines in the pursuit of *one-hundred percent* vaccination draws ideological similarities to the fanaticism of religious and political missionaries. To the religious missionary, the product that is spread and accepted is their ascribed-to deity or prophet which is often accompanied by a holy book. For a political missionary, notably the western liberating-kind, that product is their ascribed-to political ideology, i.e., democracy, and which is similarly accompanied by sacred writing or instruction. In parallel, the pharmaceutical missionary is driven to spread a divine, mankind-saving injection, i.e., covid vaccines, which accompanies with it a pamphlet and consent letter.

The ideological similarities that propel these three missionaries all center on the fundamental notion that conversion to their product, and subsequent uniformity, is the only means to personal salvation and security. It is this notion that breeds the savior-complex permeating the psyche of many vaccine fanatics. This phenomenon also helps explain not only the fervent defense witnessed towards covid vaccine mandates and passports, but the more general support for compulsory immunization. It is this savior-complex and imperialistic mindset that turns fanatic the vaccine-supporter and breeds their seemingly well-intentioned tyranny.

The theme of conversion is commonly imbedded in many religions. For example, the evangelical Christians have traditionally ascribed to the belief, as noted by the late libertarian scholar and historian Murray N. Rothbard, that the only way to fulfil their divine duty is to "maximize the salvation of others."[22] For many religious missionaries, the motivation to spread their faith and garner converts is to uphold their duty and ultimately be granted an audience into heaven. The only means for personal salvation, therefore, is attained by helping others – *the unfaithful* – avoid damnation. This is not so dissimilar from missionaries of democracy, who uphold the mission to spread their political system so as to "liberate" the people. Gathering support for their philanthropic conquest, these missionaries convince the populace that by spreading democracy, and rooting out communism and fascism, the world would be safe and free. Thus, for the political missionary, salvation, or security and liberty in this case, is attained solely by way of converting others to democracy.

This pattern follows accordingly with the pharmaceutical missionary emboldened by a savior-complex to spread vaccines to every corner of the world – as witnessed with the covid vaccine crusade. A litany of high-standing political figures, including presidents and prime ministers, broadcasted the conviction that the world must be vaccinated; that only when every human on earth is vaccinated will humanity move on from the *pandemic* and restore an existence of familiar *normality*. Klaus M. Schwab, the founder and executive chairman of the World Economic Forum (WEF) and one of the leading proponents of this cultish ideology, reiterated his belief that "as long as not everybody is vaccinated, nobody will be safe." The Association of American Medical Colleges echoed this zealous conviction:

> "[F]rom a U.S perspective, getting everyone around the world vaccinated is not an altruistic thing. It protects us here in the U.S. The side effect is that it helps everyone else around the world."[23]

What these public figures and organizations implied, as vaccine passports advocates admitted proudly, was that no one was safe and free until everyone in the world was vaccinated. These sentiments echoed throughout the covid vaccine crusade are verbatim the imperialist rationale of spreading democracy, which is designed to protect both the citizens at home and everyone else around the world. Instead of spreading democracy to stop the rise of *tyranny*, the idea was to spread covid vaccines, subsidized and mandated, to stop the rise of *mutations*. Just as it once was the obligation of god-fearing kings to spread the teachings of their deities, and as it has remained the supposed obligation of government to ironically prevent tyranny, so too is it the State's newfound obligation to ensure everyone in the world is vaccinated. The eerie parallel in these comparisons also begs the question: have dogmatic followers of "science" and compulsory vaccination simply transformed their fanatical predispositions into something more modern, progressive, and socially acceptable?

All three missionaries embody what is best referred to as *authoritarian philanthropy*, a common theme mantled by the crusaders for vaccine passports. This philanthropic authoritarianism was inherent in the "public health" mandates that compelled everyone to mask, distance, and vaccinate for the individual's own good. "Do as I say, for your own good" is the mantra for every fanatic, and covid vaccination crusaders were no exception. Supporters of domestic vaccine passports believed that vaccinating themselves was not enough. For them to be safe and free, they needed to ensure that everyone around them was vaccinated. That is why they wished for every part of society to demand vaccination proof so they could always know the vaccination status of everyone around them. This conviction to vaccinate every breathing human, as to be further discussed later, proves both dehumanizing and incompatible with the notion of liberty and consent.

In the last few decades, vaccines have begun to associate, and embody, a particular ideology which has strayed it further from its roots as a pharmaceutical product. This embodiment, or association, has turned it into a collectivist tool as witnessed with covid vaccine fanaticism. The collectivist infatuation and deification of vaccines, driven by a self-righteous savior complex, notably contributes to the distorted perceptions towards vaccines. I have hence discussed the fanaticism and distortions surrounding vaccine usage as to provide further context and explanation for both the covid vaccine crusade and its widespread compliance.

Part III:

The Ethics of Vaccine

Passports

Chapter 5

VACCINE PASSPORTS:
MORALLY INDEFENSIBLE

Being a minority, even in a minority of one, did not make you mad.
There was truth and there was untruth, and if you clung to the truth
even against the whole world, you were not mad.

George Orwell[1]

T he ethical and moral notions and consequences of domestic vaccine passports are simple yet subtle and glaring in abundance. In this chapter I dissect the nature of vaccine passports and its implications on the human existence and ordinary everyday life. The first notable observation is that vaccine passports bring forth a world where two types of humans exist: the lowly status of "unvaccinated" and the more privileged status of "vaccinated." In this dichotomy, those who refuse to vaccinate are demonized and punished while those who accept the vaccine are forced to prove their status in order to be elevated from the lowly *unvaccinated* status to the privileged *vaccinated* status. It is not enough to simply undergo a medical intervention; a spectacle must be made so as to make their act of allegiance known by means condoned by higher authority. In essence, human existence is innately treated as the undesirably unvaccinated until medically injected and consequently, by means of wearing a *badge of honour*, elevated in government-approved privileges that were once considered basic liberties.

Vaccine passports establish a government authority that embodies and monopolizes the scientific doctrine, combining State and science akin to the way the church once combined State and religion. In comparison to the State-Church alliance, a State-Science regime centered around vaccine passports produces familiar customs and notions. The State once admittedly deemed its citizens born into sin and thus were motivated to prevent the devil's influence onto the people. One way it did that was through the nationalization of education. The protestant reformist Martin Luther, a pioneering advocate for compulsory State-education, famously penned a letter in 1524 to the rulers of Germany:

> *"I maintain that the civil authorities are under obligation to compel the people to send their children to school...because in this case we are warring with the devil, whose object it is secretly to exhaust our cities and principalities."*[2]

In analogous manner, the State and its scientific ministry would view humans as born into a more secular sin: the sin of being unvaccinated. Through required immunizations in public settings, the State similarly capitalizes on State-education to ensure no child remains unvaccinated; for in this case, we are warring with a different kind of invisible enemy. To further this dystopia, the gatekeeper stationed in the ascension to the privileged vaccinated status is not only government, but the pharmaceutical industry. In another keen similarity, pharmaceutical and government bureaucrats in charge of this ascension assume the role traditionally designated for priests. That is, to absolve the sin of man in their "brutish, unvaccinated nature." The only time anyone in the past thought they could be barred from a movie theatre or museum was if they committed a crime or refused to pay the admission ticket. Alas, between 2020-2022, to be vaccinated for covid became the price of the ticket and refusal the crime.

Domestic vaccine passports both directly and indirectly criminalize the refusal of medical interventions. Without government papers alluding to the structure of your immune system, and certified by individuals in lab coats, your status as a human being is both nullified and demoted. In dystopian fashion, vaccine passports constitutionalize vaccines. In other words, they make vaccines the sole condition to exist in ordinary society. In the context of covid vaccines, vaccine passports cultivated a reality where only someone who presented mRNA antibodies had the opportunity to live their everyday life in their ordinary bodily existence. Philosopher Michael Kowalik eloquently and rightfully referred to mandatory vaccination as "discrimination against healthy, innate biological characteristics."[3] By enforcing a certain desired immune system only attained through medical alteration, naturally occurring biological traits become criminalized and demonized.

In essence, vaccine passports introduce a reality where a vaccine, as the only means to attain a particularly desired biological alteration, becomes the gatekeeper to human dignity and the means to a dignified life. Whilst these two concepts have varying conceptualizations, they are better defined as the following by the Center for Bioethics & Human Dignity at Trinity International University:

> "[The] recognition that human beings possess a special value intrinsic to their humanity and as such are worthy of respect simply because they are a human being...Thus every human being, regardless of age, ability, status, gender, ethnicity, or other status, is to be treated with respect."[4]

A dignified life can be further defined as an "opportunity to fulfill one's potential, which is based on having a human level of health care, education, income, and security" as well "the freedom to make decisions on one's life and to be met with respect for this right."[5]

Advocates of vaccine passports argued that because it was your choice to be unvaccinated, you bore the responsibility of "choosing" to abandon your dignity and to give up the expectation of being treated with basic respect. In their mind, you "chose" to be barred, by government decree, from movie theatres, museums, restaurants, weddings, fitness centres, and almost all indoor spaces that involved human congregation. Vaccine passports evidently imply that the "special value intrinsic to [one's] humanity" is vaccinated antibodies. Thus, without said antibodies, you have no *special value* intrinsic to your humanity; or at least not special enough to be allowed to coexist with other fellow humans. Such a newfound *privilege* is reserved for the *medically injected*, granted they pledge their allegiance. Vaccine passports ultimately bestow basic liberties exclusively for the *vaccinated aristocracy* in a newly formed *Pharmaceutical State*.

While there is a legal conversation tied to the undue violation of human dignity, to be discussed in a later chapter, the ethical and moral absurdity of domestic vaccine passports is readily observed. A person must undergo the known and unknown risks of a pharmaceutical product to be given the *right* to partake in *society*, fulfill a meaningful and ordinary life, and enjoy the basic dignity and respect reserved for the human race. There is, to note, nothing wrong with voluntarily undergoing risks to medical interventions, i.e., surgery or vaccination, for a perceived personal benefit. At the end of the day, we voluntarily undergo risks in every aspect of our lives, as is the reality of life on earth. The fundamental issue, however, is when consent to a risk is coerced through government-sanctioned force and segregation. It is also beyond immoral for recipients of medical interventions to be pressured to consent based on the benefits to someone else, i.e., vaccinating *for king and country*.

Another systemic consequence of vaccine passports, which favors vaccinated individuals in all facets of society, is that the system ceases to be a meritocracy. Instead, society delves into an obscure metric that judge's wellbeing, performance, and personal success by how many pharmaceutical injections a person is willing to accept. Instead of positions of employment going towards people with the skills that prove most valuable, they are filled by individuals that are most obedient to government mandates. In a private sector that is forced to adopt vaccine passports, the favorite applicant is not the one more competent but rather the one who has more vaccinations in their resume. *To be qualified is to be vaccinated*. While the world illustrated above may be seen as lunacy, it was the reality for many between 2020-2022.

In a vaccine passport-ridden society, to be around the vaccinated is deemed safe while being around the unvaccinated is considered a risk. In this dichotomy, vaccine passports treat people as sick until proven healthy and an individual that lacks vaccinated antibodies is perceived as a *public health* threat. If an individual does not have documentation alluding to their vaccination status, they are deemed dangerous and infected. This notion, imbedded into the belief that being unvaccinated is a sin, demonizes and dehumanizes the organic existence of the human species. Your human existence, in your organic state, is considered both sick and infected unless medically altered via pharmaceutical injection and proven with government certification. The notion is, however, absurd for a litany of reasons, one of them being the trillions of viruses and bacteria that exist, and spread, throughout every living organism which would consequently allude to all humans as *infected*.

To accept the notions and implications inherent in domestic vaccine passports is to live in a world that subjects humans to be judged first by their propensity to carry microscopic germs before they are judged as complex, unique, and intricate human beings. As a consequence, humans become simple numbers to be plucked into a statistical formula that assesses what risk factor they are to "public health." There are those who judge another primarily by their race, gender, sexual orientation, intelligence, and physical makeup. With the arrival of vaccine passports emerges individuals who judge others solely by their type of antibodies and their willingness to accept a medical intervention. If you have a different set of antibodies, if any at all, and or consent differently to a medical procedure, you are ostracized and demonized.

Vaccine passports, to reiterate, discriminate against individuals for their mere *potential* to carry and spread an invisible germ. Thus, such a prejudicial measure criminalizes someone for something they have yet to do. This is a slippery and dystopian hill that would lead advocates of vaccine passports to discriminate against, and preemptively segregate or incarcerate, black youth on the grounds that their demographic is statistically likelier to commit crime. I revisit this unsettling comparison later in the book.

Our humanity is imbedded in the belief that all humans possess the potential and agency for self fulfilment and actualization. In other words, we all possess the capability to live free and strive for personal achievement. With the creation of vaccine passports, the potential and agency that we all have, and the liberty to act upon it, is made conditional on the acceptance of a pharmaceutical injection. Our humanity is judged, granted, and taken away at the mercy of individuals in white lab coats and self-righteous bureaucrats. In the dystopian reality cultivated by vaccine passports, the human species is robbed of its humanity. We are not even minimized structurally, as trillions of atoms or cells that make up our body. Instead, humans are reduced to one medically injected antibody for a single germ that one may never even come across. If that is not dehumanizing, then nothing is and if this does not frighten you, then nothing will.

To further the discussion surrounding the troubling moral and ethical notions and implications surrounding vaccine passports, it is paramount to address, and rebuke, a handful of arguments that were parroted in support of covid vaccine passports. It is also time that the ideology that gave birth to vaccine passports be documented and publicly admonished. The irrationality and authoritarianism that permeates the foundation for vaccine passports will be made apparent as the ideological motivations of its handlers are broken down and illuminated.

SOCIETY AND INDIVIDUALISM

When vaccine passports were first introduced, its peddlers parroted the mantra, *"we* live in a society, it is not about *you."* Its supporters stood behind the idea that the supposed needs of the *many* outweigh the needs of the *few.* They were not shy to claim that *majority rule* ought to prevail. Their position was encapsulated by the term "social responsibility." In essence, they argued an individual ought to be denied livelihood within "society" if they refuse to abide by the dominant discourse. In cultist fashion, you were either *in* or *out.*

These advocates made clear their belief that freedom is not individual, but rather societal and thus defined by a collective.

Alas, when the freedom of the individual is defined and woven into the freedom of an imaginary whole, the individual ceases to have any freedom uniquely their own. It is no longer your freedom, but *our* freedom. It is not any longer about your health, but *our* health. It is not about you, but *us*. Collectivism attracts those who lean towards sacrificing their individual desires and needs for the safety of the hive. Within the façade of collectivism, however, its promise of safety and security become nothing more than lies.

In the beginning of the book, I discussed how collectivist ideologies have infused politically with vaccinations. Similarly, these collectivist ideologies have permeated the rationale for vaccine passports. The following collectivist viewpoints purported by vaccine advocates may stand as an argument of its own to demonstrate how we do not, in fact, live in a free society. That is, the assertions made by vaccine passport supporters would be correct if we were to accept their implicit assumption that we live under communal tyranny. Despite the dissonance, vaccine passport crusaders were entrenched in their belief that they were defending the mythically revered, *democratically free* society. To them, vaccine passports enabled this free society. After some contemplation, one comes to the realization that they in fact were right. Within the democratic society, there is seemingly no contradiction to be found in limiting freedoms as a means to protect freedom. That is how the system innately operates and the democratic authoritarians who waged war on covid exemplified this reality further. There is alas nothing "free" about a "democratically free society" and the more one ponders the phrase, which so many have grown to deify, the more Orwellian it becomes.

In the minds of those who advocate for vaccine passports, democracy is a system where they "peacefully" limit the freedom of others so as to preserve their own. This peaceful route involves enacting their will legislatively through voting. This is why supporters of vaccine passports, following the Canadian federal election of 2021, preached that "we voted for this." The perceived support of the majority gave them the reassurance that vaccine passports were morally good and anyone who objected was told to *vote* their way out in four years. In their eyes, liberty is to be gatekept behind a ballot and preserved or taken away by winning candidates. Despite the truth in their conception of democracy-in-action, they stood upon a pedestal and pretended to uphold the *constitutional democracy* that the classical liberalists had initially conceived. They preached that they were defending liberty, and the sacrosanct *free society* of the west, from the "fascists" protesting government mandates and vaccine passports. The truth I had given them credit for was a truth that even they were in denial of. In an absurd twist, they deemed those like me the enemy of liberty. The people who stood against the government's war on covid were labeled the *enemies of freedom*; it was us who supposedly distorted the meaning of being free. This grave contradiction and dishonesty on behalf of self-righteous tyrants and busybodies, is one of the many injustices that this book illuminates.

To some people's dismay, I do have not much love for democracy and have no intention of defending it, especially for what it has become. If a reckoning is to be had for those who implemented vaccine passports, it is then impossible to ignore one simple fact. The *covid regimes* were popularized in present day democracies and were most dystopian and oppressive in places that once believed themselves "free and democratic." If there is indeed a reckoning to be had, democracy must not be spared from the conversation. With that said,

I will defend the classical liberalist *dream* which vaccine passport advocates have desired to hijack and distort. In my following defense I expound the foundational principle of individualism rooted in the "free democratic society" while also critiquing the shortfalls of democracy and its increasingly apparent and perverse communistic and authoritarian elements. The latter being what vaccine passport advocates utilized in their crusade to eliminate covid-19 by any means necessary.

The collectivist assertions that were peddled by vaccine passport advocates deliberately distorted the notion of liberty. The intent of such distortion was to justify the legitimacy and morality of their corrupted creation. The foundational principle of a *democratically free society*, however, which is constitutionally entrenched in a classical liberalist ideology, contradict their collectivist distortions. The classical liberal doctrine, laying the foundation for the west's modern democratic society, set to bring forth a sacrosanct principle: individual freedom in every facet of ordinary life. This freedom was to be "guaranteed against the depredations and tyranny of the king or his minions," as Murray N. Rothbard concisely recounted.[6] Translated into more relevant language, a democratically free society, in its intentions, is predicated on the notion of protecting the individual from the wrath of an aggrandizing government and hellbent majorities who so often operate on behalf of, or in service to, the State. In parallel, this hellbent majority, operating on behalf of the government, were the peddlers of vaccine passports – who segregated their neighbours at the beckoning of government officials.

Given the sociological and political nature of the ideology inherent in the support for vaccine passports, my following rebukes passionately reference classical liberalists and libertarians alike, including the late Rothbard. It is these men, after all, who had already exquisitely addressed and refuted, more than half a century ago, the very collectivist arguments peddled once more by governments and their loyalist of subjects. To justify vaccine passports being enforced unilaterally from the top with an iron fist, supporters argued that the majority had already agreed to it and thus democracy was working as it should be. The notion that "majority rule" ought to prevail, and that the validity and legitimacy of a position is predicated on the quantity of support, is a belief farthest away from any semblance of a free society. This rationale substitutes morality for popularity and confounds oppression in the face of public support. Murray Rothbard observed this confounding fallacy half a century ago, poetically reminding the world that "crime is crime, aggression against rights is aggression, no matter how many citizens agree to the oppression."[7]

Those who advocate for democracy predicated on their preference for mob rule, however, are blinded in their own servitude. Most of the population does not, in fact, rule in any way. The *majority* does not even vote, let alone for any victorious candidate. And in any case, the majority is permitting others to rule or govern over them. In the art of simplification, the western, democratic system is better perceived as a semi-changeable oligarchy pretending to represent the *will* of the masses. In other words, democracy is a concentration of power towards a handful of individuals who act on behalf of an abstract, fictional collective. The ordinary individual who believes his desires represented or enacted by "public servants" may do well to heed the illusion of choice present in democracy and the deceiving nature of conformity.

Despite its pervasive illusions, the western democratic system is rooted, however poorly, in constitutions and charters once intended to protect the individual in three fundamental domains: life, liberty, and property. Individuals are not to be stripped of life by the hands of the State and or any aggressing individual acting either alone or in a majority. Furthermore, the supposed staple of western democracy is the championing of fundamental liberties such as freedom of speech, press, and movement. It is the right of the individual to freely speak, disseminate information, and peacefully traverse throughout the external world without undue State interference.

Alas, the error in the classical liberalist doctrine, as is the crux in Canada's democracy and the professed free society of the democratic world, is that these fundamental liberties are violated by the State in the name of *public interest*. The term "public interest," is abstract; its conception exists solely in the realm of government because it is defined by government. Thus, what *public interest* translates to is simply what the State perceives to be in the best interests of itself, which would be the collective it is deemed to embody. The extent to which government bureaucrats possess the insight to make such an impossibility possible, i.e., speak for millions of people who they have never met nor seen, is an absurdity that is rarely questioned. Nevertheless, these liberties and rights, as Rothbard precisely noted, become "tentative and relative rather than precise and absolute."[8] This crux is one of the many democratic elements that rather than free the individual, acts to imprison them. It is the crux that opens the door to tyranny and ultimately the door that enforced vaccine passports.

Moving past my ambivalence towards democracy, the initial premise of *the democratically free society*, founded upon a classically liberalist constitution, is rooted in the upholding of individualism. More specifically, it is the upholding of individual liberties in the face of tyranny. If democracy positions itself as a defender of minorities, for which it must lest it truly be nothing more than *mob rule*, it ought to defend the individual themselves. For it is to be remembered, in the spirit of Ayn Rand, that the individual is the smallest minority. The intention of the classical liberalists, in response to feudal despotism, was to create a society that emphasized individual liberties guaranteed never to be taken away, no matter how philanthropic the excuse of a tyrant was or how hellbent a fanatical mob became. What began as limited governance, however, has since grown into an increasingly bloated and intrusive government and alas the failure of the classical liberalist dream. The emergence of vaccine passports, authorized and executed by government, proved its nail in the coffin.

A prominent principle that emerges out of individualism is individual responsibility. This principle is one that is intrinsically related to the democratic ideal of self-governance and self-determination, which conflicts with the collectivist premise inherent in vaccine passports. While some may explain the concept in slight variance, individual responsibility is the extent to which individuals take accountability for their own actions, bring about their own destinies, and freely take steps to reduce their own risks in the natural world without forcefully impeding on another's autonomy or ability to exercise their own self-determination. Personal or individual responsibility is tied to each person's unique potential and capability to bring about their own fate. Without this liberty, we would be no different to puppets or machines. Individual responsibility, by the extension of free will, is the means to which humans innately operate and is illustrated in the following example. Someone allergic to peanut butter will carry an epi-pen in public instead of either forcefully prohibiting its consumption or living blindly on the assumption that everyone is, conveniently, abstaining from peanuts altogether. In summary, it is taking personal responsibility for your own life and safety without outright relying on others to mantle your responsibility either through force or blind trust.

Those most fervent in their advocacy for vaccine passports have unsurprisingly adopted collectivist notions that align with the increasingly centralized and socialist ideology of their governments. It is difficult not to notice the trend of liberalist governments becoming far more antagonistic to the notions of individual responsibility and self-governance. This antagonism is exacerbated in Canada, where increasing swaths of the populace are more than happy to give the State more responsibility, and power, to take care of them if it means alleviating responsibility off themselves.

Collectivist ideologues, running contrary to individual liberty, universally parrot the notion of "social responsibility." They argue that individuals have a "social contract" to fulfill for the "greater good of others," and that each person is "obliged to be responsible for another." These collectivist views, revitalized by proponents of covid vaccine passports, is not a new phenomenon. Rothbard observed this phenomenon in the middle of the twentieth century and notably defined part of it as "participatory communalism," where each person is entitled to own a part of someone else on the basis that nobody has ownership or responsibility over themselves.[9] That is, everyone else except oneself is entitled to dictate how that one individual ought to behave.

Rothbard also rightfully pointed out that "society" is an "abstraction that does not actually exist…there are only interacting individuals."[10] Society designates all other interacting individuals, which means when someone speaks of society, they are speaking about everyone they interact with and thus everyone but themselves. When someone wishes to dictate what *society ought to do*, they are dictating what *everybody else should do*. Murray Rothbard further noted that a fundamental error in social theory, and collectivism in general, is the inclination to treat "society" as a "superior or quasi-divine figure with overriding rights of its own."[11] This was precisely the viewpoint mantled by vaccine passport advocates who preached of *greater goods* and argued that the individual, on the basis that they live in a *society*, ought to follow the dictate of that society. In other words, these advocates believed themselves the embodiment of *society*, bestowing upon themselves the overriding power to infringe on others.

The punishment for speaking out against the "society" conjured up by vaccine passport crusaders was vilification and ostracization. For the crusaders who waged war on covid-19, the desires and dictates of their society were to vaccinate, declare vaccination status, and use the vaccine passport. Anyone who dissented to such a decree were berated and heckled to "leave society" if they did not want to "fulfill their responsibilities as a member of society." These collectivist and inherently authoritarian stances were notably embodied among a host of government bureaucrats and public health officials spearheading compulsory covid vaccination and vaccine passports.

During an Asia-Pacific business summit on November 11, 2021, Chancellor of Germany, Angela Markel asserted that individuals "have a certain obligation to contribute to protecting society."[12] Markel's statements were referencing the obligation of citizens to get vaccinated and follow covid-19 related government mandates. This *duty to society* trope was fervently peddled during the covid vaccination crusade as though it were an uncontested, divine, and universal reality of human existence. Professor Llyod Steffen, writing for *The Hill*, further espoused this collectivist rhetoric by referring to vaccination as "an obligation to society" and a "citizenship obligation" akin to conscription.[13] Chief Medical Advisor to the President of the United States, Dr. Anthony Fauci expanded upon this collectivist conviction of greater *goods* and *duties to society*, much more eloquently and ominously:

> *"You do have personal liberties for yourself. You should be in control of that, but you are a member of society. And as a member of society reaping all the benefits of being a member of society, you have a responsibility to society...there comes a time when you do have to give up what you consider your individual right. Of making your own decision for the greater good of society."*[14]

To such an obscene statement given by a government official, I nod my head in respect to Rothbard who prophetically exposed the authoritarian inclination of collectivists to utilize draconian notions of *society* as a means to override the rights of others. Rothbard may as well have been critiquing the government officials who spearheaded covid vaccine mandates and passports throughout the last two years. These collectivist and draconian conceptions of society and *social obligations* translate to an obedience to State dictate, or an obedience to government bureaucrats like Fauci, and therefore remain the antithesis to individual responsibility, self-determination, and individualism entirely. The State and its compliant herd evidently fancied themselves the masterminds in the world they conjured up for everyone else to partake in. In a display of self-righteousness, they pretended to be the spokesperson for society and mantled the position of handing down free will, atop their pedestal, to anyone who acted accordingly. In their pursuit to rid the world of covid-19, vaccine passport advocates and their government *representatives* truly fancied themselves gods.

It is also worthy to note that the collectivism preached by vaccine passport crusaders can never, without brute force, supersede the individual. This remains true, albeit tentatively, in the western "democratically free society." In a situation where the individual and the "collective" is at risk, the living and breathing individual is prioritized. As observed with covid vaccines and mandates, even during a professed *apocalyptic* pandemic, there are medical exemptions for vaccinations. Despite the perceived societal benefits, the individual's life is the utmost of importance. This prioritization of the individual is the reason blood donations and organ transplants are voluntary and require consent, as no person is forced to forfeit contents of their own body to another no matter how beneficial it is to "society." To sacrifice the life of the few, and or even just the mere individual, for any "societal good" is the end of liberty and the birth of an authoritarian regime.

The upholding of the individual's life in the face of abstract collectives is the foundation for the concept of consent itself. If *social responsibility* ever substituted the individual's ability to decide for themselves, then consent could very well be controlled by society, i.e., by everyone else. As mentioned before, this transfer of consent translates to the power and decision-making being mantled by State-approved officials. With the introduction of vaccine passports, some rightfully questioned the reality of the consent process, and whether it even existed, given the fact that consenting against covid vaccination led to government-sanctioned segregation.

To reiterate, the western, classically liberalist, democratic society is generally founded upon principles that prevent an individual from being compelled to act in the betterment of an abstract collective. I stress the word *generally*, for alongside vaccine passports, both taxation and conscription – being compulsory in nature – and other legislatively enforced "duties" rebuttal this claim. The supposed sanctity of bodily autonomy to medical interventions in western democracies is even muddied in the face of compulsory psychiatric treatment for *criminals* and the *mentally ill*. Nevertheless, it has largely remained the case in our "democratically free society" that no one is compelled to relinquish their bodily autonomy to medical interventions as a means to live a dignified life. While this protection was shaky prior to 2020, whatever truth it had left disintegrated in the face of vaccine passports.

If there is one takeaway from this discussion, it is that a collective can never be truly measured, defined, or observed and thus its draconian rhetoric treads on dangerous grounds. The individual on the other hand exists in absolute and must therefore be respected, cherished, and never preceded by the subjectivity of a "collective" being. Too many people throughout history have died at the hands of those who believed themselves the embodiment of the "greater good" and the spokesperson for their fellow brethren. This respect for the individual is evermore paramount when it involves the individuals' bodily existence and a personal decision regarding life and death – i.e., the acceptance of a medical intervention.

EXPERT AUTHORITY

The support for vaccine passports largely stemmed from a desire to uphold the dictate of "society." It was therefore unsurprising that such advocates demonstrated complete subservience to expert authority. Those who follow the dictate of society are ultimately adhering to the *intellectuals,* or experts, which mould the opinions of the masses. Those opinions held by the masses consequently become the prevailing opinion of "society." It is of no coincidence that the dominant opinions disseminated by the intellectuals and academics, throughout institution such as education and the media, echo the discourse of the presently ruling government officials. There is also no coincidence in the observation that the intellectuals who echo the will of the State are in positions of State employment, including public universities, public research agencies, State-funded media, and advisory positions within government cabinets.

What may be a coincidence for some is a deliberate manifestation of what Rothbard referred to as the "age-old alliance of the intellectuals and the ruling classes of the State."[15] The reward the State grants the intellectuals or academics for monopolizing discourse that enhances the legitimacy and validity of government policy, is incorporating them "as part of the ruling elite, granting them power, status, prestige, and material security."[16] This reality, observed half a century ago, was more relevant during the global war on covid-19 than it had ever been at the time of its writing.

The experts, scientists, and health officials that were all tasked with rationalizing and normalizing the decree of vaccine passports, among other related mandates, were both funded and employed by their respective government. The late libertarian philosopher and economist, Henry Hazlitt, prophetically expounded the tendency for institutions that are government-funded to produce government-conforming opinions:

> *"Government provide[d] free tuition…more and more threatening the continuance of private colleges and universities…tend[s] more and*

more to produce a uniform conformist education, with college faculties ultimately dependent for their jobs on the government, and so developing an economic interest in profession and teaching a statist, pro-government, and socialist ideology."[17]

In the spirit of their collectivist predispositions, peddlers of vaccine passports vilified the opinions of the ordinary individual. They considered the opinions handed down by government academics and bureaucrats as wise and factual, while the opinions of the layperson as ignorant and biased. To have disagreed or questioned the opinions handed down from the cadre of society's *greatest minds* was in their eyes an act of lunacy. In an ironic twist, they perceived those who were skeptical of the government's channel of communications, during the covid propaganda, as *indoctrinated*.

Crusaders of vaccine passports gaslit their opposition into passive compliance, towards covid-19 related government mandates, by chanting the following mantras: listen to the experts, do not think your views more valuable than the experts, and cede your voice to expert credentials. Expectedly so, the experts that these advocates were subservient towards were conveniently both government-funded and aligned with the corporate-State media narrative. The notion that the citizen ought to be subservient to the State, an ideology patriotically preached by supporters of vaccine passports, is a notion that while generally applied to collectivist thought, is particularly of fascist doctrine. Herein lies incredible irony, for it was the very people that told you to stay home and suffer the government-enforced consequences, if you were not vaccinated, who publicly labeled themselves as "anti-fascist." It was also these same people who referred to anti-government mandate and vaccine passport protesters as fascists and Nazis.

Advocates of vaccine passports undermined any individual thought or opinion that contradicted the *experts* they adhered to and, more specifically, the government decree in place. As a result, it was impossible to engage in any debate or discussion because they refused to consider information that was not preapproved by, as Rothbard categorized them, the "wise guild of scientific experts endowed in knowledge…and the arcane facts of the world."[18] These wise, scientific experts most publicized during the covid vaccination crusade, were CDC Director Rochelle Walensky, National Institute of Allergy and Infectious Diseases (NIAID) Director Anthony Fauci, and WHO Director Tedros Adhanom. It was again no coincidence that these "experts," who dictated the global covid-19 response, held positions of authority in government agencies. In a spectacle of democracy-in-action, citizens from around the world were subjected to despotic governance not only by their emergency-power hungry elected officials, but by unelected rulers' continents away.

Murray Rothbard brilliantly exposed this not-so-newfound passivity to authority; the passivity of thought and opinion induced by the State and its invested intellectuals:

> *"In the modern era, when theocratic arguments have lost much of their lustre among the public, the intellectuals have been busy informing the hapless public that political affairs, foreign and domestic, are much too complex for the average person to bother in his head about. Only the State and its corps of intellectual experts…scientists, [and] economists…can possibly hope to deal with these problems. The role of the masses, even in "democracies," is to ratify and assent to the decisions of their knowledgeable rulers."*[19]

This observation, documented half a century ago, is yet another reality that became more relevant during the government's war on covid. The years between 2020-2022 consisted of media analysts, economists, public health experts, and government bureaucrats flipping the on-and-off switch for businesses to shut down, communities to lockdown, human interaction to be regulated and outright prohibited, and events and holidays to be suspended.

Each instance that the switch flipped, a fervent army of "intellectuals" were at the ready to rationalize, justify, and normalize it to the masses. To give credit where it is due, the hegemonic system that attained widespread compliance was a force that even the greatest of those among us would have been powerless to prevent. During the covid vaccination crusade, the ordinary individual, and more broadly the masses, were induced into a state of paralysis. The on-and-off switch became such a habit that the individual was compelled to rationalize it all themselves, with the reassurance of *expert opinions*, by spouting rhetoric that granted government the absolute benefit of the doubt. "There must have been a reason" and "the government must be doing it for our best interests" were the rationalizations that brought dignity and reassurance to their compliance.

Rothbard noted this individual tendency to rationalize the coercive nature of government with the intent of remedying a cognitive dissonance. The only means for people to tolerate the omnipotence of their "public servants" is to, as Rothbard put it, believe "a dedication to altruism on the part of the State."[20] Powerless in the situation, people were compelled to adopt the belief that vaccine passports were altruistic in fear of helplessly perceiving them for what they were: coercive and forceful government intervention.

Between 2020-2022, the individual was conditioned to sit and wait until the State, and their experts, told them when it is was appropriate to close shop, wear a facecloth, keep physical distance, shake hands, gather among other humans, and traverse inside and outside their homes. The private individual, and more broadly the private sector, made a partnership with government where the leash, and title of master, was bestowed to government "health" officials. In exchange for obedience, the master promised security and safety.

Dozens of American news headlines in the latter end of 2021 declared that Dr. Fauci had green lit Halloween. In Ontario, Canada, the announcement was that the Ontario Public Health Department had signed off on Halloween. This radical deference and worship to the State in everyday life was further observed on Thanksgiving and Christmas. In 2020, government officials and hired health experts discouraged participation in the holidays, only to sign off on it the next year with dystopian strings attached. The government guidelines for the 2021 holidays included wearing masks and discerning who in the dinner table was vaccinated as to assess the windows that were to be ventilated in the room. The ordained public health officials went as far as to recommend that households refuse entry to unvaccinated family and friends.

It was a populace induced to worship the State, and live in a coma of passivity, that evidently rationalized and acted in accordance with such absurdities. A populace that embodied Mussolini's mantra: "all within the state, nothing outside of the state, nothing against the state." To anyone not under hypnosis, the reality I have hence illustrated may be mistaken for a comedy satirizing totalitarian regimes. Alas, this reality was real for those who lived through it.

"Let the *smart* and more *qualified* people upstairs run things" became the motto of the masses and taken to the utmost extreme. Individuals were not even capable of eating dinner with their family in the privacy of their own homes without the government requesting that they disclose and prioritize who in their family was masked, distanced, or vaccinated. The individual was reduced to servitude, fully at the mercy of the State and its experts who took it upon themselves to dictate the economic and social life of its *subjects*. They even had the audacity to convince the individual that it was for their own good and that they should have been thankful for it. In the face of *philanthropic tyranny*, the ordinary citizen had no power to say or do anything. Their opinion held no weight in the intellectual monopoly laid out by the government, and their academics, who defined the *will* of society. They decided what the "majority" wanted and needed and that was, conveniently, vaccine passports.

In the beginning of the book, we had spoken of the State-mercantile alliance between big business and government bureaucrats. More recently, we expounded the ideological alliance between invested intellectuals and these same government officials. Alas, these three parties collaborate within a central planning framework typical of modern democratic States. This framework is a triangular alliance that maintains ruling monopolies and hegemony in their respective societal fields: political, economic, and academic. The government in its intention to simply maintain political power and administrative godship, grants economic supremacy to its cooperative corporations and bestows academic standing for their propagandizing voices. Through this partnership, both the government, big business, and invested academics influence the social dictate of the masses.

The relationships that American conglomerate Kaiser Permanente and American consulting firm McKinsey & Company had with government health agencies that were responsible for the covid-19 response encapsulates this hegemonic State alliance and the conspiratorial influence it held on the overarching covid vaccine crusade. While the company positioned itself as a passive entity that merely followed the guidelines set by the CDC, the truth was more complex. Dr. Julie Ponesse, in her book *My Choice: The Ethical Case Against Vaccine Mandates*, highlighted the significance of Kaiser Permanente and consequently brought to light a collaboration between a conglomerate health employer and government legislation. It is this collaboration that I intend to further illuminate.

At the time that they instituted their vaccine policy, Kaiser Permanente was a prominent and influential member of the Advisory Committee on Immunization Practices (ACIP). [21] The ACIP was a committee within the CDC that focused on recommending vaccination policy to control disease-spread in the United States. While the CDC was responsible for dictating covid-19 related decrees, it did so by first endorsing the decision of its "expert" panel, the ACIP. The CDC was therefore acting upon the wishes of both academic and corporate interests. Considering the influence that the United States has on global affairs, these policies also swayed the discourse and government intervention of foreign countries, notably Canada.

There are many examples demonstrating the influence the ACIP had over the CDC in pushing covid vaccine policy. The CDC expanded eligibility of the covid vaccine boosters in November of 2021, but only after it had "endorsed the CDC Advisory Committee on Immunization Practices' [ACIP] expanded recommendation for booster shots to include all adults ages 18 years and older."[22] When the CDC expanded covid vaccine booster eligibility to teenagers aged twelve to seventeen, the CDC Director Rochelle Walensky similarly "endorsed ACIP's vote to expand eligibility for COVID-19 vaccine booster doses."[23] In declaring a clinical preference for individuals to receive the mRNA covid vaccines, the CDC similarly "endors[ed] updated recommendations made by the Advisory Committee on Immunization Practices."[24] And when the government agency signed off on covid vaccine eligibility for infants on June 18, 2022, they once again "endorsed the Advisory Committee on Immunization Practices' (ACIP) recommendation that all children 6 months through 5 years of age should receive a COVID-19 vaccine."[25]

In every instance of U.S. policy change regarding covid vaccines, the will of the ACIP was endorsed and consequently the desires of its leading members, which included conglomerate employer, Kaiser Permanente. The same employer who, following their vaccine mandate policy, cried out that they were simply following government dictate. The employer, Kaiser Permanente was not however alone in its collusion. Other corporate delegates sat on the ACIP throughout 2020-2022 with a similar motivation to coercively increase covid vaccination rates. One such member who sat on the committee was the CEO of Franny Strong Foundation, a non-profit organization with a mission to "boost childhood immunization rates for all vaccine-preventable diseases."[26] The foundation also publicly upholds the belief that when immunization rates drop, "the public health of the entire region, state, and nation is threatened."[27] As much as these corporations benefited financially, the covid vaccine crusade was evidently a war propelled by collectivist ideology.

McKinsey & Company, a global management consulting firm headquartered in the U.S., discretely partnered with a litany of governmental agencies to assist in the public response to covid-19. Some of the firm's clients during the global covid vaccine crusade included the pharmaceutical company Pfizer, international organizations such as the WHO and Melinda Gates Foundation, and the governments of

France, United States, Ontario, and Quebec. While the World Economic Forum, an international lobbying organization, is not a client, McKinsey considers them a strategic partner for which they engage in frequent collaborations. The WEF have an admittedly fascist or corporatist agenda, which is to strengthen "public-private cooperation" for the "global public interest." In other words, a partnership between governments and corporations for the betterment of the State – or the *greater good*.

The World Economic Forum also has a related program named "Young Global Leaders," which is a list of individuals that have been recognized for making positive global change and who have seemingly engaged with the WEF. On that list is French President Emmanuel Macron, New Zealand's Prime Minister Jacinda Ardern, and Canada's Prime Minister Justin Trudeau. Considering these three government officials were among the leaders of the covid vaccination crusade, what the WEF considers "positive global change" is telling. McKinsey's strategic affiliation with the WEF is important in the following discussion if only to highlight their shared ideological framework and motivations as well as their social networking circle.

An investigation published by *Radio-Canada*, originally released in Canadian French and translated through *Google Translate*, revealed that "McKinsey played a central role in the game plan for the vaccination campaign in Quebec, drawing on its experience with other states."[28] The firm was also responsible for aiding the Quebec government with the decision surrounding "the lifting of COVID-19 pandemic slowdown measures."[29] In France, the firm was noted as "the keystone of the vaccine campaign."[30] Governments around the world, including prominent international pseudo-government authorities such as the WHO, essentially employed and funneled millions of taxpayer money into a multinational corporation which they hired to help orchestrate, and cultivate compliance towards, the covid vaccine crusade. The firm also recommended that governments around the world reach "an agreement with the manufacturer Pfizer."[31] Through the firm's collusion with government agencies, McKinsey served the interests of its corporate client, Pfizer, who gained preferential treatment particularly in Canada as the only authorized vaccine at the start of the vaccine campaign.

Conglomerate employers, partnering with governmental agencies, and driven by ideological and financial motives, played a substantial role in creating public policy surrounding covid-19. It is imperative to mention that these policies, which advanced the production and distribution of covid vaccines, notably crippled smaller businesses while bestowing unprecedented profits for larger companies. The government's war on covid unequivocally and unsurprisingly benefited big business. Canada's Emergency Wage Subsidy created to "remedy" the hardships that emerged from repeated lockdowns and restrictions between 2020-2022 is one of many examples. According to the Canadian government agency, *Statistics Canada*, the majority of the one hundred-billion-dollar relief program that was originally tooted for small businesses, primarily went to large corporations.[32]

The CEO of the Canadian Federation of Independent Business, Dan Kelly, as a reaction to this revelation, remarked that the "government has had a profound misunderstanding of how small business works."[33] While I concur that incompetence is innate to government bureaucrats, such disparity was far more deliberate. The government has a far better understanding of larger corporations because it is precisely them that they preferentially serve. After all, it is not smaller businesses who spend millions annually to lobby and curry favour with government officials.

The case of Kaiser Permanente and McKinsey & Company are one of many examples of big business collaborating with government and their cadre of hired public academics and experts to implement policy and legislation. In this case, the policy was related to the distribution and acceptance of covid vaccines which ultimately translated to the birth and enforcement of vaccine passports. The lack of concern or media coverage surrounding these hegemonic, conspiratorial collaborations of "expert authorities" exemplified the subservience towards expert-led government decrees during the covid vaccination crusade.

FREEDOM TO COMPLY

"You know what? If you don't want to get vaccinated that's your choice, but don't think you can get on a plane or a train next to vaccinated people and put them at risk," the Prime Minister of Canada, Justin Trudeau, declared during a campaign speech in Winnipeg on August 20, 2021.[34] Atop their pedestal, peddlers of vaccine passports claimed that the individual had the *freedom* to refuse the covid vaccines but not the freedom to avoid the *consequences*. The consequences that included being marginalized socially, mentally, and financially. These crusaders smirked in their boastful and profound assertion that *you* had the freedom not to follow the rules, outlined by them, but not the freedom to avoid the consequences similarly outlined by them. Given the authoritative tirades by the layman conformist, one might have thought they made the rules. On the contrary, they were simply obeying and parroting the decree of their respective rulers. It was the conformists who were most adamant about the necessity to conform.

Their slogan was simplified down to the following phrase, "actions have consequences." While a universal and common phrase, its rationale in the context of covid vaccine passports was nothing short of draconian. After all, it was the ones imposing the consequences that delivered such condescending and authoritative rhetoric. The people who were not marginalized by the vaccine passport, predicated upon their compliance and obedience, were understandably content to repeat such draconian consequences with boastful immunity.

In response to protests that criticized vaccine passports and mandates, it was common to overhear covid vaccine crusaders heckle from the sidewalk three overused slogans: "Have fun losing your job," "I look forward to seeing you on the ventilator," and "just get vaccinated." When these were the statements echoed from one side to another, it was apparent which side was the aggressor. In response to refusing a medical injection, the covid vaccination crusaders berated your character and wished to rob you of all integrity and bodily autonomy. In their egotism, advocates of vaccine passports believed themselves intelligent with their choice to be complicit in the ultimatum the government had provided them. The ultimatum that compelled covid vaccination and the use of vaccine passports to gain the privileges of living an ordinary life. They evidently confused their cowardice and obedience with bravery and honour.

To parrot the phrase "actions have consequences" in the context of vaccine passports is nothing more than classic authoritarianism. It is akin to a child punching another at recess for making fun of them.

That was the "consequence," after all. In the same analogy, a by-stander may speak the phrase – a third child watching the ordeal absent the courage to stand up to the aggressor. This bystander per-spective was more accurate to the reality that transpired, where many felt helpless to prevent vaccine passports and thus resorted to mere silent compliance. The claim that an individual had the free-dom to refuse vaccination but not the freedom to avoid its punish-ment was simply a draconian justification for vaccine passports. While supporters of vaccine passports were victorious in some of their goals, their success said more about the failing of liberalist con-stitutional democracies.

The "consequence" for an individual's action that does not con-stitute a crime, i.e., consenting against a medical procedure, was never supposed to legally, nor morally, impede on their basic human rights. The "action" of exercising one's inalienable right to personal auton-omy, self-determination, and consent to a medical intervention was never supposed to illicit the wrath of what came with vaccine pass-ports. The mere refusal of a pharmaceutical injection was never meant to strip a person of basic liberties to live an ordinary life and freely interact with other individuals. Despite the fact that all of this transpired when few ever believed it possible, there is no victory to be won for the side that watched their creation burn down whatever trust people had in the promises of their deified democratic society.

WAR ON GERMS

"Being coughed on…is not my idea of freedom. Those refusing a vaccine must face the consequences. The rest of us have rights too, including the right to life," Associate Editor of the Independent, Sean O'Grady proclaimed on May 18, 2021.[35] In their war on covid-19, its crusaders ushered a greater war on *germs*. They were vocal in their conviction that people ought to be morally and legally protected from the transfer of germs and, ultimately, from sickness itself. Mantling the iron hand of the State, they sought policy and police enforcement to prohibit individuals, deemed a public health risk, from entering societal spaces and congregating amongst other humans. Unsurprisingly, they exclusively targeted individuals who were either unvaccinated, defiant to vaccine passports, or failed to be *fully vaccinated*.

While their intention was to prevent the transfer of one single germ, however impractical that was, the creation of vaccine passports barred human interaction entirely and thus translated to the prevention of all germ-transfer. Advocates of vaccine passports humorously claimed that no one had the right to infect them and went as far as to suggest that such a right be amended into their respective constitution. They believed the statement, "you have the right not to be infected," should be inscribed within the promise of life, liberty, and security of persons. The war on germs rhetoric further championed the notion that others had the right to refuse vaccination but not the right to be around them and make them *sick*. This impractical and dehumanizing view of humanity, regurgitated by the hellbent masses, were infamously echoed on national television by a host of government officials, notably Dr. Anthony Fauci. In an interview with ABC, Fauci stated the following:

> *"If you get infected, even if you are without symptoms, you very well may infect another person...so in essence you are encroaching on their individual rights because you are making them vulnerable."*[36]

It is paramount to remember that the likes of Fauci vilified the act of breathing as they accused ordinary and innocent people of making others vulnerable by doing absolutely nothing but existing in their human body. Anthony Fauci further perpetuated this fear-mongering and dehumanizing rhetoric when he recommended everyone to indiscriminately get tested when gathering in each other's homes and avoid "gatherings where there are people who you do not know what their vaccination status is."[37] In other words, avoid human beings that have not had their immune system altered through a particular medical procedure.

These arguments and the rationale behind them, whilst dystopian, remain nothing more than symptoms of germaphobia. The *war on germs* rhetoric justified the advocacy for vaccine passports by normalizing both the paranoia and contempt towards the unvaccinated. Their hysteria was capsulated by the remarks of Barry Mehler, a tenured professor at Ferris State University. In protest to in-person classes, Mehler had this to say in his introductory video posted online to the class on January 9, 2022:

> *"No liberty (expletive) of an administrator is going to tell me how to teach my class… so if you want to complain to your dean, (expletive) you… Go ahead, I'm retiring at the end of the year, and I couldn't give a flying (expletive) any longer. You people are just vectors of disease to me, and I don't want to be anywhere near you."*[38]

Alongside perceiving the unvaccinated as "vectors of disease," advocates of vaccine passports presented a double standard towards their vaccinated peers. While they feared the unvaccinated, they did not criminalize nor fear the vaccinated spreading covid-19 among other germs and diseases. "You only have a right to infect others, *if you are vaccinated"* was what they inherently implied. This rationale is scientifically absurd. As I mentioned before, we have trillions of viruses and bacteria inside and outside of our bodies that we transfer to others every second of every day. There is no right to pass or not to pass on germs, as it is as naturally occurring and uncontrollable as the sun rising and setting. It is not the right of the sun to do so, it simply does so. To attempt to regulate such a natural and invisible process would be lunacy, as demonstrated through 2020-2022.

At the end of the day, we may very well all be perceived as "vectors" for disease. This basic reality is largely the reason no one is held criminally responsible when someone is infected with influenza, strep, mono, bronchitis, and other coronaviruses to name just a few. No one is also criminalized for knowingly and or unknowingly passing on germs to others in ordinary everyday life. Outside of the technical legal reasons as to why this is the case, the practical explanation is that if germ transfer were criminalized everyone would be immediately jailed. If anyone can find historical precedence for the outright criminalization of basic germ transfer, I am confident the origins of its rulings are rooted in a eugenics era or within a totalitarian regime. Prior to the emergence of vaccine passport crusaders, it would have only been totalitarians and eugenicists who would have the self-righteous audacity to indiscriminately obliterate liberty by regulating human anatomy in the name of collective safety.

Those who adopted the *war on germs* ideology essentially advocated for the State to outright regulate and penalize human interaction with germs and, as a consequence, human interaction itself. Given our coexistence with trillions of germs and other microscopic organisms, advocates of covid vaccine passports more broadly advocated for the State to regulate the biological contents of the human body. Inherent in the notion of vaccine passports, its supporters would evidently desire government to be both the master in mind, body, and spirit. This rhetoric rang a familiar tune with State eugenics, which can be defined as a State-sanctioned desire to control and regulate human interaction, and ultimately human bodily existence, all in the name of collective preservation.

A poor counter deployed by vaccine passport advocates pertained to the legality of some sexually transmitted infections (STI), notably HIV. The precedent that some governments have set towards the non-consensual transfer of an STI was sufficient justification to penalize germ-transfer in the context of covid-19. This justification extended to the segregation of the potentially infected which happened to only be the unvaccinated. There are, however, a few things to be said to this disingenuous argument. First, the criminalization of sexually transmitted infections is not universal, and the mere fact that some governments believe themselves authorized to meddle in the sexual activities of consenting adults is troublesome in and of itself. Nevertheless, the legal rationale surrounding STI's pertains not specifically to the germ transfer itself. Instead, the crime is related to the breach of consent in the context of a sexual act. Proponents of these laws argue that refraining to inform a sexual partner of your sexually transmitted disease would be breaking consent laws and thus akin to sexual assault. The *right* not to pass on germs is not applicable, nor is it ever mentioned, as it would be incredibly difficult to prove in most scenarios.

The relevance of the argument is also absent. The criminalization of the transference of STI's is not remotely comparable to simply walking and breathing in the streets and transferring germs in an ordinary humanely fashion. Nowhere in the law, as it pertains to the non-consensual transfer of sexually transmitted infections, does it grant justification to penalize the individual for breathing. To reiterate, the technical and overarching reason there exists no definite law for the general transference of germs is because the act of transferring any one germ is not an intentional act. Without diving into the concepts that define criminality, the *war on germs* rhetoric, which called to criminalize germ transfer and constitutionalize the right not to be sick, was laughably absurd.

SMALLPOX VACCINATION

Earlier in the book we had discussed the distorted recollections pertaining to vaccines and their overstated significance in human history. In those discussions, I highlighted the exaggerated impact that two vaccines had on the reduction of both diphtheria and pertussis occurrence and mortality. There is another vaccine, however, that has become fabled in the psyche of modern society; and that is the smallpox vaccine.

The international ten-year vaccine campaign that started in 1967, orchestrated by Donald Ainslie Henderson, led the World Health Organization to declare smallpox eradicated in 1980. Alas, the *success* of the smallpox vaccine spelled out decades of justifications for compulsory vaccination. The covid vaccine campaign was no exception. Advocates of covid vaccine passports had the story of smallpox at the ready for every confrontation. Not only did they use it to argue for mandated covid vaccination, but they utilized the smallpox story to guilt their opposition. Consistent with their ideology, supporters of covid vaccine passports accused anyone who was against vaccine mandates as wishing for children to die. Anyone who was against making covid vaccines compulsory was also deemed a hypocrite because they or their parents supposedly conformed during the smallpox vaccine campaign. They argued that mandates for the smallpox vaccine helped eradicate the virus and it was therefore justified to do the same with covid vaccines. To them, coercion begot coercion. The problem with this justification, however, is that the success of mandatory smallpox vaccines is misleading and overstated. Whatever impact the vaccine and its related policies had on smallpox, its significance does not warrant the worship it receives in public discourse nor its influence on compulsory immunization.

While smallpox did, for the most part, disappear following the ten-year global campaign, the significance of the smallpox vaccine and its mandates were heavily overstated. In line with what is often omitted from the stories of vaccine success, mortality from smallpox started to decline in Europe as early as the nineteenth century before smallpox vaccines were readily distributed. One prominent case study to examine is twentieth century England, which eradicated smallpox with a uniformly unvaccinated population that favored the Leicester method.

The Leicester method was led by *antivaccinationists* in response to compulsory, or mandated, smallpox vaccination. The method originated in the industrial town of Leicester and rose to popularity after its efficacy in combating the smallpox epidemic of 1892-1894 with a uniformly unvaccinated populace. Their success was put on further display when the town's performance was compared to highly vaccinated neighbouring towns, like Warrington and Sheffield, who fared far worse during the epidemic. Proponents of the Leicester method dissuaded from smallpox vaccination in lieu of other measures including quarantining the sick and increased sanitation. Leicester was supposed to be a plague-ridden town, but the contrary had occurred – and it was in no credence to the smallpox vaccine nor its mandate.

By the middle of the twentieth century, compulsory smallpox vaccination was abolished in England and the English population, who were uniformly unvaccinated at the time, became officially untouched by smallpox. One revealing excerpt that elucidates the mythical tale of the smallpox vaccine comes from Dr. G. K. Bowes observations of England in 1946:

> *"Its decline in the later decades of the nineteenth century was at one time almost universally attributed to vaccination, but it is doubtful how true this is. Vaccination was never carried out with any degree of completeness, even among infants, and was maintained at a high level for a few decades only. There was therefore always a large proportion of the population unaffected by the vaccination laws. Revaccination affected only a fraction. At present the population is largely entirely unvaccinated. Members of the public health service now flatter themselves that the cessation of such outbreaks as do occur is due to their efforts. But is this so? The history of the rise, the change in age incidence, and the decline of smallpox rather lead to the conclusion that we may here have to do with a natural cycle of disease like plague, and that smallpox is no longer a natural disease for this country."*[39]

American author and journalist, Arthur Allen, documented a similar observation in his book, *"Vaccine: The Controversial History of Medicine's Greatest Lifesaver."* Allen noted that while the smallpox vaccination rate in England was upwards of fifty percent in 1914, its rate dramatically decreased to eighteen percent in 1948.[40] Kristoffer Mousten Hansen, a research assistant at Leipzig University, concisely illuminated the fictional story of the smallpox vaccine at a time when it was being weaponized by advocates of covid vaccine passports:

> *"Public health and vaccination programs rest on one central story: that they were crucial to the elimination of one of history's greatest killers, smallpox. As we've seen, this is not true: vaccination was never universal across Europe and North America…and the decline in mortality and the disease disappeared at the same time everywhere in the Western world, despite whatever variations in public health policies there were. Even countries such as England that had de facto given up on compulsory vaccination were rid of the disease…The official history of smallpox is a main support for the policies of modern health authorities. If it is exposed as largely mythical, the central ideological justification for compulsory vaccination falls by the wayside."*[41]

The bubble of the seemingly impenetrable smallpox fairytale has been briefly fleshed out and exposed in more honest detail. Whether the smallpox vaccine mandates "worked," however, is irrelevant to the issue at hand. Coercion remains coercion despite the benefits that are reaped. Even if the story were true, and that the vaccine and its mandates successfully eradicated the virus, the smallpox vaccine had notoriously fatal and injurious side effects that were not rare in the slightest. It is readily acknowledged that upwards of one thousand people for every one million experienced serious adverse reactions to the smallpox vaccine, and fourteen to fifty for every million experienced fatal reactions.[42] No such product or anything of the like should ever be coerced onto the population, let alone by their governments.

This coercively imposed risk is also why the city of Leicester protested in 1885 against mandatory smallpox vaccinations, holding slogans that read "The Three Pillars of Vaccination – Fraud, Force,

and Folly."[43] The smallpox vaccines were not only being proved ineffective to limit the cycle of smallpox epidemics, but the populace
began to acknowledge the risks associated with the injection. Advocates of compulsory covid vaccination failed to comprehend that
compulsion breeds resentment. Leicester citizens demonstrated this,
nearly two centuries ago, as they proudly protested mandatory vaccination with another famous sign that read "Liberty is Our Birth-
right, and Liberty We Demand."[44] The crusaders for compulsory
covid vaccines, who were determined to trade every ounce of liberty
for a false sense of security, erroneously believed the cries of freedom
and protest they witnessed, in opposition to their authoritarian mandates and passports, was a phenomena new to humanity.

The tale of the smallpox vaccine used by advocates of vaccine
passports to justify their coercion was evidently flawed. The position
that supporters of vaccine passports mantled was also a mere imitation
of the authoritarianism that citizens centuries ago fought against in
the name of liberation. Proponents of mandatory covid vaccines
tried to convince everyone that the smallpox vaccine saved humanity and that everyone took the vaccine happily because they were
caring and altruistic people. They were also vocal in their conviction
that without individuals surrendering their freedoms of bodily autonomy to the government, smallpox would plague our societies to
this day. As we have come to learn, none of that is true.

SCHOOL IMMUNIZATION

In another attempt to irrationally justify the existence of vaccine passports, notably in Canada, its advocates turned to school immunization.

They notoriously undermined the outcry towards vaccine passports because they perceived it as no different to school immunization, which they believed were mandatory. They rationalized vaccine passports by reminding themselves and others that they were *forced* to vaccinate as children, and they followed it up by telling themselves and others that "it was just a vaccine." With their logic, government mass surveillance would be *just a camera.*

They essentially used the precedent of child and school immunization to gaslight opposition and normalize the sweeping requirement of covid vaccines throughout society, i.e., vaccine passports. In America, its advocates cited a 1922 Supreme Court ruling, led by Chief Justice Melville Fuller, which upheld state-school entry vaccine requirements.[45] The 1920's was the peak of the eugenics era in the United States and thus it was not a surprise that courts at the time ruled in favor of granting the State authority to enforce medical procedures in order to be educated. The moral significance or weight of this cherished precedent is further diminished by the fact that a decade before, Melville Fuller upheld Louisiana's Jim Crow legislation that required racial segregation on its railway trains.[46] Misattributing significance to precedent was a common theme among those who were desperate to garner historical support for their advocacy of vaccine passports.

In the following analysis of Canada's immunization policies, I intend to rebuke the premise and rationale of this justificatory rhetoric – particularly as Canadians regurgitated it. The 1996 Canadian National Report on Immunization explicitly states that "immunization is not mandatory in Canada" and that it "cannot be made mandatory because of the Canadian Constitution."[47] The report also declares that "legislations and regulations must not be interpreted to imply compulsory immunization."[48] These sentiments, stated directly from the Government of Canada, remain true to this day and thus any mention of "mandatory" or "compulsory" ought to be thrown out entirely from this discussion.

The initial purpose of requiring proof of immunization for schools was not to disallow or bar those who refused. Instead, it was to *aggressively* remind parents that have forgotten to immunize their children and to require parents whom object to "actively refuse and sign documents attesting to that fact."[49] In other words, it was meant to make parents who dared refuse vaccination walk through hell to stand by their conscience. Ontario is one of two other Canadian provinces that require up-to-date vaccination to attend schools. In the provisions, however, there are medical, religious, and conscientious exemptions. Parents who object on conscientious grounds have, however, recently been forced to attend a vaccine education session i.e., a form of re-education camp. A public health official is even deployed to confirm, or interrogate, the parents to ensure they watched the "video education session." Despite the soviet inspired tactics, child immunizations in Canada are evidently not mandatory nor have they ever been.

Even if vaccinations were mandated for children in government schools, however, such an act would nevertheless be both immoral and irrelevant to the subject of vaccine passports. School immunization policies do not justify the government-sanctioned segregation and ostracization of those who utilize their autonomous right to refuse a pharmaceutical product. The reality that government health agencies could forcefully remove children from government schools for refusing a pharmaceutical product is also not very becoming of our self-declared "free" society. The premise of using school immunizations to justify vaccine passports also infantilizes the adult population, treating society as if it were an elementary school. By equating government officials to school administrators and citizens to students, its advocates make a mockery of the "democratic and free" society they worship. This infantilization of adults was a common theme among peddlers of vaccine passports who proudly called for a helicopter government to protect everyone from themselves.

TRAVEL REQUIREMENTS

The crusaders for covid vaccination, known by the moniker *covidian*, further attempted to justify covid vaccine passports by convincing others that they were always forced to vaccinate, and or show proof of vaccination, in order to travel overseas. Thus, akin to child and school immunization, they saw no difference between travel requirements and societal or domestic vaccine passports. The premise of this justificatory rhetoric was similarly both flawed and irrelevant. When it comes to travel requirements, the only vaccines required by a very minute selection of countries include ones for polio, yellow fever, and meningococcal. The requirements are also selectively enforced for individuals traveling from high-risk areas, as determined largely by the World Health Organization.

Most of the countries that, in specified situations, enforce vaccine requirements include China, Saudi Arabia, and Pakistan. The vaccine requirements for polio and yellow fever, however, only apply to travelers who originated from a high-risk area. This distinction excludes most people from any such "requirement." It does not apply to most people in the west, including Canadians and Americans.

Despite this reality, covid vaccine passport advocates who resided in the west erroneously parroted the belief that everyone was required to vaccinate to travel abroad. The argument of justifying covid vaccine passports through travel requirements is evidently both dishonest and misleading. However, even if it were true, their argument suffers from hypocrisy and irrationality. The covidians who jumped on travel requirements to justify covid vaccine passports suffered from the fallacy of precedence, which plagued every excuse to normalize vaccine passports.

In plain language, this fallacy refers to the erroneous granting of legitimacy to a current measure or way of existence predicated solely on the basis that something similar was tolerated and or existed in the past. This rationale is referred to as a fallacy on the basis that the past does not innately justify the future. Abuse in the present moment is not suddenly tolerated simply because it had occurred or been tolerated in the past. In other words, just because something exists or had existed does not solely justify its current existence or expansion. Ironically, this book highlights the dangerous precedent, and subsequent slippery slope, that vaccine passports may set in motion. Paradoxically, it was school compulsory immunization, existing travel restrictions, and historical vaccine mandates that became precedence for the acceptance and normalization of covid vaccine passports. The very thing they tried justifying through precedent therefore exposed the problematic nature of accepting something merely because something similar had existed in the past. Alas, every atrocity committed against groups of people throughout history has been deceptively rationalized and justified by some form of precedent.

Supporters of vaccine passports justified mandatory covid vaccination through travel requirements and in doing so they deceptively equated covid-19 to more harmful diseases. Meningococcal for example, in a study of older hospitalized patients, had an overall fatality rate of twenty five percent. [50] This is drastically different to the mortality rate of covid, even among immune-compromised seniors. Not only is meningococcal more severe than covid-19, but its vaccine is almost exclusively recommended. Advocates of vaccine passports therefore weakened their position by bringing up mostly recommended vaccines, for higher fatality diseases, to justify mandatory vaccination for covid.

The nature and mortality of covid-19, for essentially all age-groups, is more comparable to modern influenza. Therefore, a more reasonable comparison would be between covid and the flu. In the conversation of travel vaccine requirements, however, a comparison with influenza was fervently avoided because it exposed their hypocrisy. In their efforts to normalize compulsory covid vaccination through established vaccine requirements, they were silent on one fact. The influenza vaccine remains absent as a requirement to travel overseas, despite the virus infecting one billion people[51] and contributing to the passing of up to six-hundred and fifty thousand people[52] annually. When you consider how long influenza has been in circulation, the question ought to be asked: why were those who crusaded for the covid vaccines silent on the absence of flu passports and mandates?

Given how empathetic covidians were in their heartfelt slogan of "all deaths matter," you would think they would have advocated for flu passports and lockdowns during influenza seasons a long time ago. Prior to their crusading efforts beginning in 2020, they were silent on influenza passports, season-related lockdowns, and mask mandates. They seemingly accepted influenza as part of human life for decades, only to suddenly rise in hysterics towards covid-19. It became clear that covidians only crusaded for the covid vaccine passports because it was their way to "do their part" and show allegiance to their government. None of their rationale, or arguments, were consistent because it was all a case of broken telephone.

The attempt to utilize modern-day travel requirements to justify societal, or domestic, covid vaccine passports was egregiously irrational. The ability to entertain a shoemaker business in one's own neighbourhood or country of residence had no relevance to whatever bureaucratic foreign policy requirements existed for international travel. Nor did a vaccine requirement for traveling to a country like Zimbabwe or France hold any relation to a mother dining at a nearby pizza joint with her son and daughter. The ability for a child to enter school, or an adult to attend post-secondary education, similarly had no connection to a person traveling to a Caribbean resort for a one-week vacation. Akin to their previous arguments, the premise of using vaccine travel requirements to justify domestic vaccine passports, and more specifically freedom passports, was factually incorrect and lacked any semblance of relevancy. One may even argue that this justification ironically delegitimatized their own support for compulsory covid vaccination both abroad and domestic.

ABUSER ULTIMATUM

The notion that covid vaccine passports were needed to prevent hospitalizations rose to popularity among covidians following the failure of the vaccines to eliminate covid transmission. That was, after all, what people were promised would happen when they accepted lockdowns and waited for the vaccines. Once that proved to be a farce, the covid crowd argued that rising hospitalization led to lockdowns and therefore vaccine passports, by way of reducing hospitalisation, were the only route to avoid further lockdowns and restrictions. While they boasted in their supposed altruism for the *collective good*, their position was irrational, dishonest, and nefarious.

Hospitalizations do not naturally beget lockdowns. The notion that reaching hospital capacity justifies intrusive and invasive government intervention, i.e., lockdowns, is nonsensical and authoritarian. Hospitals naturally reach near or full capacity throughout the year due to several reasons including alcohol-ramped holidays and adverse weather. Overcrowded hospitals are considered a normal tradition, and this is especially true with Canada's socialized healthcare system. In Canada, excessively long wait times are commonplace for healthcare appointments including general admission, surgery, checkups, and treatments.

Traditionally, there has never been mention of an inevitable lockdown as a result of a bad influenza season or any other time that saw hospital capacity reached. Even in the 1976 swine flu epidemic such rhetoric was absent. During the 2018 flu season in the United States, Alabama declared a state of emergency; a medical center at New Jersey was declared "at capacity," and California hospitals treated patients in tents.[53] Despite this particularly bad flu season not too long ago, the notion of societal vaccine passports and lockdowns ceased to exist – until the year 2020.

The belief that hospitalizations begets lockdowns and vaccine passports, begs a fundamental question that its advocates never bothered to answer. And that question pertains to why governments would punish citizens, socially and financially, for being sick and admitting themselves into hospitals that are designed to treat them. Hospitals are literally funded to care for the sick and its staff are paid by customers who desire medical care. In other words, why are people punished for using a service they pay into? A problem of infrastructure should never scapegoat, demonize, and imprison the individual. Covidians insisted on decreasing hospitalization to the lowest possible denominator before agreeing to revoke their beloved vaccine passports. It was as if they believed hospitals were meant to be empty and favored bankrupting them.

When did it, however, become the responsibility of government bureaucrats to prevent people from requiring hospital treatment. If that is the government's newfound duty, then they ought to ban driving, unhealthy eating, drinking, and smoking. If eliminating risk in life is their new objective, they should ban living entirely. With that said, lockdowns are the closest thing to a prohibition on living. If not for their salaries diminishing, I am certain covidians and their newly representative government officials would truly be content with eternal lockdowns coupled with a virtual existence.

The hysteria towards patient admissions into intensive-care-units (ICU) and the obsession with reducing ICU numbers, as though having ICU's being used were a terrible thing, was as irrational as their wish for hospitals to be empty. ICU space has always been generally low, particularly in Canada, given the costs of operating beds. According to a 2016 report by the *Canadian Institute for Health Information*, "the daily cost of an ICU stay is as high as 3 times that of stays in general hospital wards across Canada."[54] The panic of ICU's nearing or reaching capacity was similarly nonsensical when confronted with reality. Among large hospitals in urban areas, which account for the majority of ICUs, bed capacity is often exceeded.

In Canada, ICUs operate at about ninety percent capacity with frequent periods of overcapacity.[55] The reality of limited, crowded, and growing ICU numbers is not unique to Canada, or any other developed western country with a socialized healthcare system and an aging population.

Supporters of vaccine passports cultivated a taboo surrounding hospitalization, which led to the problematic notion that hospital beds were designed for certain people. This created a mutual blame-game, perpetuated by governments and their funded media. State-corporate media blamed the unvaccinated covid patients for taking up space that should have been used for patients of other ailments. At the same time, they blamed patients of other ailments, such as alcoholics, for "blocking" beds that were apparently meant for covid patients.[56] Hospitalizations were grossly politicized by bureaucratic officials threatening lockdowns and prioritizing certain afflicted populations. This politicization deliberately contributed to the unvaccinated being demonized for seeking treatment in a facility that was once promised to treat them indiscriminately.

Governments that introduced vaccine passports as the alternative to lockdowns, at the sight of "overcrowded" hospitals, essentially imposed a draconian ultimatum. An ultimatum that was shamelessly peddled and defended by the *covidian* crowd. They argued that it was either vaccine passports or lockdowns and nothing in between. Anyone who opposed vaccine passports was accused of wanting the populace to be subjugated to lockdowns. The crusaders who peddled this rhetoric desired the populace to accept the *lesser evil* they had provided.

The ultimatum placed upon the people, between segregation or lockdown, was the embodiment of abuser behaviour. The abused partner, being the ordinary citizen, was convinced to accept the torture ensued by vaccine passports because the worse outcome – lockdowns – were graciously spared by the benevolence of their abusive government officials. The citizen dared not complain about vaccine passports for they did not wish to be placed in yet another lockdown. To further the gaslighting typical of abusers, the abused citizen was instructed to be grateful for the treatment they were given because it was done for their own good and to save their life.

This abusive benevolence, or philanthropic tyranny, was a common theme among the peddlers of compulsory covid vaccination and one that I have made emphasis to unsparingly expose. In Canada, this abusive rhetoric was notably espoused by the following: Prime Minister Justin Trudeau, Health Minister Jean-Yves-Duclos, and Deputy Premier and Minister of Health Christine Elliott. When Trudeau announced a federal proof of vaccination certificate, he called on the Canadian populace to get vaccinated as it was the only "way we can all get back to the things we love [and] avoid further lockdowns."[57] Jean-Yves Duclos, reminding the populace of the ultimatum between vaccinating or living with lesser freedoms, regurgitated this *benevolence* when he defended the federal airline ban that remained on the unvaccinated:

> *"The reason for which we can rollback some measures is because we have a high rate of vaccination…we cannot choose to have public health measures rolled back if we do not have the right rate of vaccination."*

The duration of lockdowns in Ontario were divided into stages, requiring the populace to reach certain vaccine uptake thresholds or milestones in order to take back some of their freedoms. As the government of Ontario cheerfully announced that some of its restrictions were easing due to the population's compliance and performance,

Deputy Premier Christine Elliot announced the following on February 17, 2022:

> *"Thanks to the province's high vaccination rates and the continued sacrifices of Ontarians, we are now in a position where we can move forward in our plan earlier than anticipated…With hospitalizations and ICU admissions continuing to decline we are committed to maintaining a gradual and cautious approach to protect our hospital capacity."*[58]

To paraphrase, they could not let up their abuse until they were satisfied with the "right rate" of obedience. Victims of abuse are often shamed for opposing their injustice, and so too did the covid vaccine crusaders berate and shame anyone who opposed lockdowns and vaccine passports. Anyone who dared oppose the government's *philanthropic abuse* was labeled anti-mask, anti-vax, and anti-lockdown. They were accused of wishing hospitals to collapse and people to die in the street. The wish for voluntary action and choice was deemed too dangerous for the emergency-authorized tyrants and their loyal crusaders. *Choice was not an option when lives were at stake,* they said.

A NECESSARY EVIL

None of the arguments for vaccine passports ever really *argued* for a vaccine passport. They were simply a means for its supporters to erroneously justify and coercively normalize their use. A societal freedom passport, predicated on vaccination status and orchestrated with the global technological orthodoxy of the modern world, was never trialed in the history of mankind. It was never trialed until the year 2021. The lack of morally consistent and rational arguments for vaccine passports was therefore expected. Even for some its own supporters, vaccine passports were considered, in response to "unprecedented times," a *necessary evil*. It was nonetheless an evil and admittedly so.

The lack of foundation for vaccine passports, alongside a plethora of reasons, was rooted in the disconnect between what it pretended to be and what it was. In other words, it was built on lies and perpetuated on even greater lies. Vaccine passports pretended to be a "public health" measure with a goal that was "based in science." However, neither its existence nor function held any rationale or supportive evidence. Covid vaccine passports were simply modern-day internment camps: State enforced segregation in times of *emergency*, driven by fear and irrationality. The internment camps of the twentieth century are considered today a dark period in human history, and so too will vaccine passports suffer the same fate.

Whether it was the quarantine hotels that housed the unvaccinated in Canada; the quarantine camps that kept the unvaccinated in Australia; or the unvaccinated Italian islanders that were barred from entering the mainland, covid vaccine passports led to the worst kinds of imprisonment. The numerous incidents of segregating and fining the unvaccinated alas garnered popular support. However, the support witnessed towards covid vaccine passports was not a new phenomenon. The most erroneous of internment camps in the twentieth century received popular support at the time. The segregation of Jews into the ghettos of Germany also gained popular support within German society for it was framed as a public health response to typhus outbreaks, which were deceptively blamed on Jewish communities. The masses in democratic societies tend to initially support every government action because of the illusion that permeates every democracy. Governments supposedly represent the people and thus what the government does the people naturally are inclined to support. The alternative, in theory, would be to ask people to oppose the will of themselves.

On the subject of government encampments, it is relevant to highlight the findings from a CDC assessment of a strategy that involved physically isolating unvaccinated individuals. In July of 2020, the CDC evaluated a strategy of housing or "shielding" unvaccinated individuals within certain communities. The government's report was titled *"Interim Operational Considerations for Implementing the Shielding Approach to Prevent COVID-19 Infections in Humanitarian Settings."* While the strategy itself is unimportant, the criticisms that were highlighted by the CDC illuminate the hypocrisy of government "health" agencies and the injustice of covid vaccine passports.

The significance of the critiques, which were directed towards the shielding strategy, was that they applied in parallel to vaccine passports. Despite the similarity, however, governments spearheaded vaccine passports on the recommendation of the CDC and other omnipotent government agencies. The CDC report outlined various criticisms towards the strategy of isolating or shielding unvaccinated individuals within camps or community settings. Some of the issues that were highlighted involved the approach appearing *forced* and that the forceful separation would lead to the following:

> *"[R]isk of stigmatization…feelings of isolation… [and] significant emotional distress, [which would] exacerbate existing mental illness or contribute to anxiety, depression, helplessness, grief, substance abuse, or thoughts of suicide."*[59]

The criticism by the CDC towards the shielding strategy concluded that "isolating individuals and limiting their interaction, compounded with social and economic disruption...raised concerns of potential increased risk of partner violence."[60] These concerns and critiques were eerily identical to the ones directed towards the "strategy" of covid vaccine passports. While vaccine passports and the "shielding strategy" were somewhat different in context, their consequences played out in kind. The isolation ensued by vaccine passports led to consequences that included stigmatization, emotional distress, and disruption within the family. It is easily argued that the CDC-sanctioned strategy of vaccine passports, considering they were a form of nationalized and global segregation, had far worse of a negative impact than the shielding strategy of isolating the unvaccinated within humanitarian camps. Ironically, the latter was deemed too harmful and psychologically abusive by the CDC.

How is it that the shielding strategy was not only criticized but abandoned while vaccine passports were adopted and enforced unilaterally is a mystery driven by malicious motivations of coercion and heavy-handed government overreach. As to be highlighted in the following chapter, all the ethical and moral concerns that were brought up against covid vaccine passports were ignored and dismissed in the name of coercively increasing vaccination uptake. Their coercion was all in the name of *science*

Chapter 6

VACCINE PASSPORTS:
THE SCIENCE

One of the defects of contemporary culture is the undue and un-healthy reverence we show toward scientists. The public imagines scientists to be too smart to disagree with, too objective to be swayed by emotion or bias, and experts on every subject they choose to talk about. None of these things is true, of course.

Chris Clemens[1]

This chapter is dedicated to the science, or lack thereof, regarding vaccine passports as to further highlight its ethical and moral injustice. I labeled this chapter "The Science" in reference to the peddlers of vaccine passports who deified and trademarked the word "science" to both validate and enforce their position as well as defend it from opposition. *The Science* proved them right and any opposition was consequently deemed inconsistent with their trademarked science. As touched upon previously, science had been deified and highjacked, by the crusaders of covid vaccines, to resemble God. They were proven correct not by *the word of God* but rather *the word of science*. The strategies of the ruling powers to garner support have remained steadfast throughout the centuries. The only difference is that semantics have changed to fit with the progressive times of the present century.

Medical masks as a garment to be worn in everyday life was once a non-existent notion, particularly in the west. The consensus had been that there was little inclination towards its effectiveness or its economic and ecological practicality. Alas, at the turn of 2020, this consensus and subsequent reality that had persisted throughout the centuries ended abruptly. Government mandates for mask-use rolled out globally and has become normalized to the point that it is still, to this day, either recommended or mandated globally. The slogan for mask-use, which circulated in newspapers and media outlets, simply read: *"The Science Changed."* The science had changed suddenly and in accordance with the objectives of the State. So too, when vaccine passports rolled out had the *"The Science Changed,"* in favor of the government once more. Supporters of vaccine passports and their government-clothed shepherds obsessively clung to this dogmatic perversion of science. Thus, it was unsurprising that vaccine passports had not a shred of scientific data or rationale to justify their immoral existence.

This chapter is dedicated to exposing the scientific contradictions and subsequent irrationalities inherent in covid vaccine passports. In highlighting these contradictions, I further illuminate the moral indefensibility of vaccine passports. The scientific contradictions and irrationality of vaccine passports stemmed from three related phenomena: the covid vaccine did not in fact prevent transmission, natural immunity conferred protection longer than initially purported, and the unvaccinated were not exclusively transmitting covid nor were they more at risk of death. The covid vaccine booster campaign is documented in this chapter as to further expose the dystopian reality of vaccine passports and the inefficacy of the covid vaccines.

COVID-19 TRANSMISSION

The covid vaccines did not prevent contracting or transmitting the virus despite the lies first purported by government institutions. CDC's Director Rochelle Walensky, infamously proclaimed in an *MSNBC* interview on March 29, 2021, that "vaccinated people do not carry the virus [and] don't get sick."[2] It was based upon these lies that led many to parrot the "pandemic of the unvaccinated" rhetoric. While once disputed, the reality that vaccinated persons spread the virus associated with covid-19 became universally recognized. On August 6, 2021, the CDC released an internal document that found "vaccinated individuals infected with [covid-19] may be able to transmit the virus as easily as those who are unvaccinated."[3] Following this study, Rochelle Walensky publicly backtracked in an interview with *CNN*, when she announced that "what they [the covid vaccines] can't do anymore is prevent transmission."[4] This initial "ground-breaking" observation was reinforced in the mainstream by a paper published in the Lancet Infectious Diseases medical journal, which found that vaccinated persons were just as likely to spread covid to contacts in their household as those who were unvaccinated.[5]

The early studies of 2021 primarily mentioned the covid-19 variant known as *Delta* for it was the dominant strain globally at the time. The covid-19 strain *Omicron* that succeeded the delta variant turned out to be even more prevalent and evasive to vaccine immunity. *Forbes* even reported on May 13, 2022, that "immunity against omicron coronavirus variant fades rapidly after a second and third dose of Pfizer BioNTech's Covid-19 Vaccine."[6] The following subvariants of the omicron strain that rose to dominance in the spring of 2022, proved to further "evade protection from vaccines...more easily than most of its predecessors."[7] This timeline is important if only to merely highlight the overarching failure of the covid vaccines, and its accompanied crusade, to prevent what they were initially purported to accomplish.

Before a litany of published studies highlighting the lack of efficacy of covid vaccines made the truth more palpable to broadcast towards the masses, the facts were observed in real-time as cases among vaccinated skyrocketed. Among an array of examples, Cornell University reported nine hundred and three covid-19 cases in the second week of December 2021. Cornell's vice president for University Relations, Joel Malina, confessed that "virtually every case of Omicron variant to date has been found in fully vaccinated students, a portion of whom had received a booster shot."[8]

On December 21, 2021, the world's biggest cruise ship experienced a covid-19 outbreak despite a sweeping requirement that compelled everyone aged twelve and upward to be fully vaccinated.[9] Following the outbreak, the CDC warned the public to avoid cruises even if vaccinated. The peddlers of vaccine mandates and passports found it difficult to blame the unvaccinated children on the ordeal considering the fact that ninety five percent of the passengers on board were vaccinated and among the people who tested positive on the ship, ninety-eight percent were "fully vaccinated."[10] In line with the intended function of vaccine passports and its related policies, the unvaccinated were imprisoned in their homes and barred from cruise ships because transmitting germs and contracting covid was a privilege and freedom bestowed exclusively to the vaccinated.

At the turn of 2022, the reality of covid cases among the vaccinated became the new norm. However, this reality existed the moment vaccine passports were implemented. The new variants simply gave people an excuse to blame both the virus and the unvaccinated. The coercive and authoritative mandates would have worked if only it was not for the virus, they rationalized. *If only everyone got vaccinated*, they cried. Two publicized examples in the sports industry that made a mockery out of vaccine passports were witnessed within both the National Football League (NFL) and the National Basketball Association (NBA). Even though the league had instituted a vaccine mandate, they experienced a covid outbreak that was considered "out-of-control."[11] To remedy the situation, the NFL mandated boosters for all its players and staff. The NFL's mandate to be double vaccinated, which was what the term "fully vaccinated" meant before boosters arrived, was so arbitrary and ineffective that they mandated everyone to be triple vaccinated. The denial among covid vaccine fanatics were on display for the world to see.

The Brooklyn Nets, a basketball team incorporated into the NBA, shamelessly instituted a vaccine requirement that suspended their player Kyrie Irving who refused to be vaccinated. The suspension did little to change his mind, and after months of prohibiting his involvement in the team and watching exponentially rising covid cases between vaccinated individuals, both around the world and within the NBA itself, the team backtracked their decision and allowed Kyrie Irving to play. However, as a result of the New York City vaccine mandate which at the time had yet to be rescinded, Irving was forced to sit in the audience and watch his team play while in the city's stadium. The segregation was blatantly apparent at this point in time and thus was even picked up by the mainstream media. Following heightened pressure, New York City dropped one of its many mandates and Kyrie Irving was finally allowed to play basketball without second-class treatment for refusing a pharmaceutical injection.

The government's war on covid-19 did not have any shred of scientific integrity, which explains why in the beginning of 2022, despite the observable evidence, many governments expanded vaccine mandates and increased crack downs on the unvaccinated "fraudulently" using vaccine passports. During heightened covid-19 cases among the vaccinated, the problem apparently stemmed from the unvaccinated mother using a fraudulent passport to enter campus to visit her child. *The problem clearly did not lie with the passports themselves.* The war on drugs, terror, and poverty failed in spectacular fashion, and it is evident that the war on covid will suffer the same humiliating fate.

As governments were eventually forced to change their rhetoric, so too did the crusaders for covid vaccines. They went from the belief that the vaccine prevented covid-19 to the belief that it *reduced* the likelihood of contracting or transmitting covid. This change of rhetoric followed the lead of the CDC and other government agencies who argued that the covid vaccines "can reduce the spread of disease."[12] The tentative nature of such a statement, however, and the inability to define what reduction and spread entailed were all glaring issues among advocates for mandatory covid vaccinations.

Even if we were to believe the CDC's refined claim that the vaccine may have reduced spread, the extent to which it may have theoretically *reduced* contracting or transmitting the virus was irrelevant. That is, because it admittedly did not *prevent* either. This was initially apparent with the delta variant before it became undeniable with the following covid strains including omicron, which was ironically first identified within the United States in a vaccinated individual.[13] Given the failure of the covid vaccines to prevent transmission, the CDC ended up encouraging covid vaccination by claiming that the vaccine "significantly lower[ed] your risk of severe illness, hospitalization, and death if you g[ot] infected."[14]

The ending narrative of the covid vaccination crusade, which hampered evermore their justification for vaccine passports, was that covid vaccination were mere symptom mitigators. Alas, they now pretend the narratives they peddled prior never existed; that they never pushed for compulsory covid vaccination in order to reach *herd immunity*, predicated on the belief that it prevented transmission and *suffocated* the virus from the community. Despite the sequence of failed and crumbling narratives, governments and their covidian infantry remained resolved to blame everything on the unvaccinated. The State-corporate media perpetuated the vilification, likening unvaccinated individuals walking in public to driving "on the opposite side of the road"[15] and labeling the unvaccinated as "super-spreaders" and "variant factories."[16] Its crusaders were convinced they failed in their objective because they did not convert enough of the unvaccinated.

Domestic vaccine passports evidently cultivated a reality where only vaccinated persons in public could spread germs, including covid. This was the manifestation of their phrase "you have no right to infect others, unless you are vaccinated." Unvaccinated individuals were disallowed from societal spaces because they would hypothetically transmit covid-19 while vaccinated persons, who could similarly transmit the virus, were allowed to freely roam in public. This facet of vaccine passports, and the overarching covid vaccine crusade, was the epitome of hypocrisy and discriminatory segregation.

Advocates of vaccine passports justified this hypocrisy through their cultish devotion to the belief that that unvaccinated *spread more*. However, no quantity of dehumanizing generalizations and convoluted probability formulas of fictional possibilities could have prevented the inevitable. That is, to allow into an establishment a vaccinated person infected with covid-19 while barring an unvaccinated person who was covid-negative. Alas, this inevitably was the reality of vaccine passports which ought to be remembered in history as an unprecedented display of State-sanctioned biomedical segregation.

NATURAL IMMUNITY

The covid vaccination crusade was built upon the lie that the human body was incapable of developing immunity to covid-19 without the aid of vaccination. Some of its crusaders convinced the public that natural immunity only lasted for a few weeks. Despite these initially purported lies, a consensus evidently developed around the subject of natural immunity to covid-19. The consensus was that antibodies developed naturally after a covid infection conferred robust and durable protection to future reinfection.

On October 15, 2021, the Brownstone Institute for Social and Economic Research published an article that outlined, for the first time, one-hundred and six studies that affirmed naturally acquired immunity to covid-19.[17] The following timeline illustrates a few of these studies as to emphasize and document the scientific confidence that developed in relation to naturally acquired covid-19 immunity. A paper published in the journal *Lancet* and conducted by researchers in Denmark, found that "natural infection with [covid-19] led to observed protection against reinfection estimated to be approximately 80% after 6 months."[18] A medical Op-Ed titled *"Quit Ignoring Natural Immunity"* authored by Dr. Jeffrey Klausner and Dr. Noah Kojima, noted that Epidemiologist's estimated on May 28, 2021, that "160 million people worldwide have recovered from Covid-19 [and] those who have recovered have astonishingly low frequency of repeat infection, disease, or death."[19] This observation of covid-19 severity and mortality remain unchanged in 2022.

In relation to durability, a research paper published in the journal *Nature*, found compelling evidence that covid infection in people "robustly establishes the two arms of humoral immune memory: long-lived bone marrow plasma cells and memory B cells."[20] In plain language, natural immunity to covid conferred long-lived immune cells which implied long-lasting and prolonged protection. A highly publicized preprint study, conducted by researchers in Israel and published in the summer of 2021, popularized the confidence that had developed around natural immunity.

Researchers in the Israeli study demonstrated that "natural immunity [to covid-19] confers long lasting protection and stronger protection against infection, symptomatic disease and hospitalization" in comparison to those with "vaccine-induced immunity."[21] Another prominent study, published by the CDC, collected case data from over a million individuals who tested positive in New York and California between May and November of 2021.[22] The researchers found that the unvaccinated who had natural immunity were more protected than the vaccinated population that were never infected. Ironically, vaccine passports and mandates were the most intrusive and widespread throughout cities in both New York and California.

The contention on whether natural immunity was superior or not in respect to covid-19 remains irrelevant. The issue of discussion is not that of "science," but that of choice and morality. Coercing anyone to vaccinate, including those who garnered natural immunity, is not only a moral violation but a violation of medical ethics. This blatant violation was further exposed following the publication of a study in *Nature* on January of 2022. The paper demonstrated that antibodies produced from other coronaviruses, including the common cold, protected against covid-19 infection as well as reduced the risk of contraction.[23] This finding not only strengthened the moral defense against compulsory vaccination, but it further rebuked the narrative that vaccination was the only means to attain immunity towards covid-19.

The coercive goal of one-hundred percent vaccination uptake, spearheaded by the erroneous conviction that compulsory injection was the *only* way to end the *pandemic,* was an ethical violation even among mainstream medical standards. Coercively administering the covid vaccination onto those who had some natural immunity, whether to covid-19 specifically or other coronaviruses, was an unnecessary form of medical intervention. The covid vaccination also exposed individuals to further known and unknown risks associated with the medical procedure. To reiterate, vaccine passports, which coerced everyone, regardless of whether they had naturally acquired immunity or not, into vaccinating was scientifically egregious and morally unjustifiable.

BOOSTER CAMPAIGN

Research has indicated that covid vaccination and repeated boosters may have a negative effect towards established natural immunity. One such study found that a second dose of the mRNA vaccine "results in a reduction of cellular immunity in COVID-19 recovered individuals" which suggested "that a second dose, according to the current standard regimen, of vaccination, may not be necessary in individuals previously infected with [covid-19]."[24] Two unsettling implications came out of these studies as it pertained to both the nature of vaccine passports and the overarching crusade.

Most vaccine passports adopted throughout the world, particularly in Canada, ignored natural immunity and, as a consequence, compelled even those who had recovered from covid-19 to vaccinate. Vaccine passports also required strict adherence to the regimen of "fully vaccinated," which at the beginning of its rollout meant two doses of the covid vaccine. With the arrival of the booster campaign, however, that requirement expanded to include boosters, or additional doses. Individuals were therefore compelled to risk their lives with consecutively required injections as well as potentially damage their own naturally built immunity. This section documents the global booster campaign in order to illustrate the unsettling reality of the covid vaccination crusade as well further illuminate the injustice and dystopian nature of vaccine passports.

Dr. Anthony Fauci remarked in December of 2021 that changing the definition of fully vaccinated to include booster shots was a matter of "when, not if."[25] Shortly after he made the statement, Fauci announced the replacement of "fully vaccinated" with keeping your vaccinations "up-to-date."[26] To be fully vaccinated thus meant to be updated on all the boosters that were required by the government. Intent on leading the booster crusade on all fronts, Dr. Fauci, in an interview with *CBS News* on December 30, 2021, made this emphatic remark:

> *"If you are not boosted, get boosted. What is called by definition, or legal, or other purposes, a 'fully vaccinated person' is, in fact, irrelevant. If you want to be fully protected, get boosted. I am saying it very loud and very clear right now."*[27]

The booster campaign in Britain was spearheaded by their Prime Minister, Boris Johnson, who made this hypnotic appeal on December 12, 2021, with the arrival of a new covid variant:

> *"Let's Get Boosted Now. Get Boosted Now for yourself, for your friends and your family. Get Boosted Now to protect jobs and livelihoods across this country. Get Boosted Now to protect…our freedoms and our way of life. Get Boosted Now."*[28]

Anthony Fauci's partner-in-crime, CDC Director Rochelle Walensky made a nationally televised plea to reignite the booster campaign in the United States during a White House press briefing on July 12, 2022:

> *"Many Americans are under-vaccinated, meaning they are not up to date on their covid-19 vaccines. Not all people over the age of fifty have received their first booster dose [and] of those who received their first booster dose only 28% of those over fifty have received a second booster dose, and of those over 65 only 34% have received their second booster dose…It's essential that these Americans, as Dr. Jha said, get their second booster shot right away."*[29]

In Canada, Trudeau made public his pledge towards expanding the covid vaccine crusade when he reassured Canadians that the "boosting vaccination campaign" was among his government's priorities in 2022.[30] Following on his promises, Trudeau secured thirty-five million boosters for 2022 and thirty million for the year 2023 as well as an option for sixty million doses in 2024.[31] Canada was not, however, alone in its pursuit of an endless booster campaign and subsequent "forever war" with covid-19. Netherland's health minister, Hugo de Jonge, similarly purchased covid vaccine boosters into the year 2023 with the goal of reaching "six vaccine booster doses."[32]

The *booster crusade* ushered in a fear of mandated annual covid vaccines, both in Canada and throughout the world, which prominent figures and institutions remain determined to translate into reality. When covid vaccine mandates and passports were first being implemented globally with indefinite deadlines, Pfizer's CEO Albert Bourla, on September 26, 2021, made public his hopes that "we will have a [covid] vaccine that you will *have to* do once a year."[33] The "philanthropist" Bill Gates provided further support to the "forever booster hypothesis" in an interview with *CNN* on May 13, 2022:

> *"[T]o be safe, every six months you are probably going to be vaccinated... As we get more data, they might even make that shorter for people who are sixty or over seventy where the duration seems to be a bit lower...we are in for ongoing vaccination to stay absolutely safe."*[34]

Canada's Health Minister Jean-Yves Duclos, during a press conference on July 4, 2022, eerily declared that "we will never be fully vaccinated against covid-19...two doses are not enough; we need to maintain our vaccinations up to date."[35] In his speech, Duclos defined being "up to date" as having "received your last dose in the past 9 months," implicating an annual requirement to vaccinate.[36] Governments around the world, particularly in Canada, culminated a reality of dystopian proportions as they unabashedly demanded its citizenry be annually "updated," with the latest purchase, as though they were software.

The idea that vaccine passports would require compulsory annual injections, or boosters, was initially dubbed a conspiracy theory. Alas, as it is often the case, the once labeled conspiracy theory first turned into reality on January 24, 2022. That is, when France officially required its citizens to attain a booster or third vaccine dose for their vaccine passport to remain valid. However, a month before the presidential election on March 14, 2022, France suspended their vaccine passport. The tune of elections had a significant impact on the "science" of covid-19 for a host of countries who backtracked, one after another, on their vaccine mandates.

Despite mandates around the world being reluctantly relinquished and suspended, the global booster campaign and the overarching covid vaccine crusade remains persistent to this day. On July 19, 2022, *TIME* magazine published a headline that read, "Why You'll Need to Get COVID-19 Boosters Again and Again,"[37] exemplifying the continued efforts to normalize what they once dubbed conspiracy – *forever boosters*. The upcoming introduction of *new generation* covid vaccine boosters to combat new coronavirus mutations only further cements in truth what was once censored. It remains apparent that the fears of living in this reality, where freedoms are yearly renewed through adherence to a pharmaceutical product, is a fear that shall persist so long as there exists those who advocate for vaccine passports.

A litany of public and private institutions were notable accessories to the government's dystopian booster campaign. In December of 2021, over twenty-five universities and colleges in the United States required their students to get the booster shot to be enrolled.[38] In Canada, during the fall of 2022, the University of Toronto mandated covid boosters specifically for resident students[39] and the University of Western Ontario instituted a sweeping mandate that required covid boosters for all enrolled students.[40] A row of Wall Street firms, including leading global investment business Blackstone Inc., prohibited their employees who were not boosted from working in the office.[41] In Victoria, Australia, over four hundred and twenty public school teachers were terminated following their refusal to receive both the covid vaccine and its booster shot.[42] The people were once promised that after two doses they would have their lives back. Alas, as wholly expected from tyrannical ultimatums, two doses were not enough to have the freedom to pay for an education, be regularly employed, and or simply live an ordinary life.

An ethical and moral consequence of the booster campaign, which called to vaccinate the unvaccinated and "boost" the "unboosted," was that it introduced a new human tier within vaccine-passport ridden society. The lowly unvaccinated and the privileged vaccinated tiers made acquaintance, two years into the government's war on covid, with the "unboosted" population. The latter group was simply anyone who was not *up to date* on their boosters and as a result had their "fully vaccinated" license revoked.

In the *Pharmaceutical State* birthed by vaccine passports, people were expected to renew, alongside their driving licences, the contents of their immune system. In this case, the renewal involved the acceptance of a government provided pharmaceutical injection. Akin to driving without insurance, the punishment for disobeying the renewal of your immune system, and thus walking in public without certification, included fines and criminal charges. Those who accuse me of hyperbole likely never paid attention to the television or the "newspaper of the internet," i.e., the State-funded media headlines curated on the front page of all corporate search engines.

If they had tuned into the digital matrix, they would have readily observed the dystopia first-hand. *The Atlantic* was one of the first to publish an article that questioned if "unvaccinated little kids [could] safely spend time with [an] unboosted adult?"[43] The mainstream American magazine even referred to our times as the *"Booster Era."*[44] The reality between 2020-2022 was determined to create a dystopia that put George Orwell and Aldous Huxley to shame.

THE VINDICATED

If the intent of vaccine passports were to protect the unvaccinated, as dishonestly argued by some of its advocates, then the notion was scientifically absent. An unvaccinated young person was less likely to be negatively affected by covid-19 compared to a vaccinated senior, a vaccinated person with obesity, and a vaccinated individual who had compromised immunity. This sentiment was echoed by the John Hopkins University School of Medicine, which proclaimed that "many people infected with the coronavirus do not feel sick or have only mild symptoms."[45] This was especially the case among younger populations who were statistically unscathed from covid-19 irrespective of its differing strains.

The polling firm *Impact Research*, who declared itself a "proud pollster for President Joe Biden" and a "proud ally and asset to progressive causes and campaigns," emboldened the parallel between influenza and covid-19. In a memo sent out on February 24, 2022, the firm stated that "what most Americans are dealing with" is a "disease with fatality rates like the flu."[46] Humorously, this statement technically violated the "covid-19 misinformation" policies of the mainstream social media platforms. YouTube's covid policies prohibit content that claims "COVID-19 is less severe or equally as severe as the common cold or seasonal flu." Facebook's covid-19 policy similarly prohibits any claim that states "COVID-19 is no more dangerous to people than the common flu or cold." The democrat polling firm, however, received no backlash or censorship, likely due to their affiliation with certain ruling parties and ideologies.

The reason covid-19 is compared to influenza and why vaccination is largely irrelevant to the subject of its severity is due to the similarly discrepant mortality rates between age groups. According to the data provided by the CDC in November of 2021, mortality for covid-19 in comparison to the age group of 18-29, was four times higher between the ages of 30-39 and 370 times higher in individuals 85 and older.[47] CDC Director Rochelle Walensky solidified this discrepancy when she stated the following, in reference to a study[48] of 1.2 million vaccinated Americans, during an interview with *ABC News*:

> *"The overwhelming number of death [to covid-19], over 75 percent, occurred in people who had at least four comorbidities… so really these are people who were unwell to begin with."*[49]

David Grabowski, a professor at Harvard Medical School, echoed the acknowledgements and subtle concessions made by the CDC:

> *"[The] bulk of deaths among older adults are those oldest old. So they're individuals aged 85 and older. They're individuals with comorbidities, cardiovascular disease, obesity, diabetes. They are also typically individuals living in nursing homes."*[50]

Vaccination was not the sole and key denominator of covid severity, and to have treated it as such was dishonest. *The Washington*

Post, who was notoriously hellbent on vilifying the unvaccinated following the covid vaccine rollout, even acknowledged, in April of 2022, that "new data underscores that age – even with vaccination – is a massive risk factor for covid death."[51] This information was readily made available prior to the implementation of vaccine passports but alas the admissions and confessions were postponed until after the populace was coerced to vaccinate. The reason for such delay was due to the fact that vaccine passports were never rooted in any honest measure of science. Instead, the covid vaccination crusade was propelled by the self-righteous belief that the government ought to forcefully *help* individuals against their will.

The philanthropic tyranny that characterized the support and enforcement of vaccine passports was proudly boasted by State institutions and government officials. The *OSHA* justified enforcing its federal covid vaccine mandate as a way "to protect the unvaccinated employees," from themselves, as they "face[d] grave danger."[52] Another notable admission came from Quebec's health minister, Christian Dube, who proudly declared that "if they [the unvaccinated] can't protect themselves, we will protect them against themselves."[53] The blatant authoritarianism and covid fearmongering was a playbook that government's exploited for as long as they could.

In a society characterized by this authoritarian philanthropy and made possible by an omnipotent government ruling over a docile populace, vaccine passports intent on protecting the *vulnerable* would segregate or imprison groups deemed high-risk. These groups would include seniors and those with underlying health conditions such as obesity or cancer. It would be nonsensical for governments to segregate healthy teenagers and adults because they refused a State-provided injection. The only reason governments would ever segregate healthy, unvaccinated individuals is if the intention were to merely punish disobedience and coerce the consumption of a desired product. The latter was what had evidently transpired.

Supporters of vaccine passports notoriously clung to the view that the unvaccinated were infected and walking plagues of sickness. This perspective, however, was not only unscientific but illogical and germophobic. The fact that individuals could provide a negative covid test or proof of natural antibodies was not enough reassurance for the covidian crowd. To partake in their world, you had to harbour spike-protein vaccine antibodies. Even with vaccine passports that did provide alternatives, the rationale and subsequent hypocrisy was blatant. Considering vaccinated individuals could contract and transmit covid, it would only make sense that they would join the unvaccinated in requiring a negative test. Alas, the vaccine passports that provided alternatives compelled only the unvaccinated to display daily testing results, exempting the vaccinated from such a rule. The vaccinated were able to walk freely as human beings even if they contracted covid-19; a privilege not given to the unvaccinated.

To this hypocrisy, passport advocates found no issue. Their lack of dissonance was the case because the sole reason the unvaccinated were exclusively required to undergo testing was simply to *not punish the vaccinated for doing their part*. When negative tests were first required indiscriminately of vaccine status for travel and hotel quarantines, the covidian crowd was outraged. In response to media and "expert" backlash, many of the requirements were dropped for the vaccinated as to *not punish them for vaccinating*. The requirements remained for the unvaccinated merely to "incentivize" them to vaccinate. Incentivizing vaccination uptake was evidently both the means and the ends of the covid vaccine crusade.

When covid cases, particularly among the vaccinated, fluctuated upwards in the late months of 2021, sweeping testing requirements around the world were temporarily reinstated. The United Arab Emirates, for example, only allowed "boosted" citizens to fly out of the country, leaving out the unboosted who were once privileged in their "fully-vaccinated" status.[54] This transfer of privilege was to incentivize more vaccination uptake even among those already vaccinated. However, to not disincentivize vaccination during the booster campaign, many governments reduced quarantine times for anyone vaccinated. It was a trade-off in a carefully devised incentive strategy. In totalitarian fashion, privileges and rewards replaced any conception of natural rights and what followed was continued obedience to maintain conditional liberties.

The premise of a societal *freedom* passport that is tied to vaccination status; to a certain antibody presence; and to the willingness to undergo a medical injection, is scientifically and morally absurd. Alas, the existence of vaccine passports were unaffected by a lack of scientific and moral reasoning for they required none. Its sole objective was simply to coerce the increase of vaccination uptake. That is all that mattered. When vaccinations increased, both the government and the *covidian cult* paraded in the streets, overlooking the calamity that had birthed its achievement.

The mental, financial, and social pressure accompanied by the segregation was the forefront of vaccine passports. The government's covid-19 interventionist policies that turned the world upside down, which included vaccine passports and lockdowns, were a classic case of the "ends justify the means." As the Leninist saying goes, to make an omelet you ought to break a few eggs. In order to

The Science

get one-hundred percent vaccination rate, the State similarly had to break a few of its subjects. Science was evidently not the driving force of vaccine passports and therefore scientific reasoning was futile to oppose it. The lack of covid vaccine efficacy, the existence of natural immunity, and the vindication of the unvaccinated meant nothing to the crusaders of vaccine passports. The quest for truth and the upholding of morality had no place in a conversation of coercion and force.

Chapter 7

VACCINE PASSPORTS:
THE LAW

When law and morality contradict each other, the citizen has the cruel alternative of either losing his moral sense or losing his respect for the law...There is in all of us a strong disposition to believe that anything lawful is also legitimate. This belief is so widespread that many persons have erroneously held that things are "just" because law makes them so.

Frédéric Bastiat[1]

To conclude the ethical discussion of vaccine passports, this chapter expounds on the legal foundation of moral principles egregiously undermined by vaccine passports. The moral-legal principles that are notably violated include voluntary consent, human dignity, and a host of constitutional rights typical of western democracies and or republics.

VOLUNTARY CONSENT

Vaccine passports fundamentally undermine voluntary consent by gatekeeping liberties behind the acceptance of medical interventions.

That much this book has hitherto made apparent. In bringing to light the legal writings that uphold such an inalienable component of liberty, this section further exposes the extent that covid vaccine passports obstructed the sacrosanct right of voluntary consent. *The Universal Declaration of Bioethics and Human Rights*, describe medical consent as:

> *"Preventive, diagnostic, and therapeutic medical intervention...*
> *[which includes medical injections] ...carried out with the prior,*
> *free and informed consent...and may be withdrawn by the person*
> *...without disadvantage or prejudice."*[2]

One of the most prominent international human rights documents, *The Nuremberg Code*, further codifies the requirement for voluntary consent to be exercised freely "without the intervention of any element of force, fraud, deceit, duress, over-reaching, or another ulterior form of constraint or coercion."[3] While the charter rights in violation are expounded in more detail at the end of the chapter, *The Canadian Charter of Rights and Freedoms*, among other present day constitutions bedded into western democracies, have generally been entrusted to uphold the right to exercise choice in refusing a medical treatment without disadvantage or prejudice.

The *Canadian Medical Protective Association*, an organization incorporated by an Act of Parliament, upholds the position that all medical and surgical treatments, involving a patient, adhere to the fundamental principle that "every human being of adult years and of sound mind has the right to determine what shall be done with his or her own body."[4] The Canadian organization also emphasizes that all patients "must be free to consent to or refuse treatment" and that "consent should be obtained without duress or coercion" which includes ensuring that "no one else has imposed their will on the patient."[5] Canadian physicians are also legally liable "in assault and battery for physically touching or treating a patient when no consent was given" and that includes "treatment beyond or deviating significantly from that for which consent was given."[6] Canadian law in theory may have once upon a time admirably prioritized medical consent. Alas, Canada will forever be remembered as spearheading the creation and enforcement of covid vaccine passports and related mandates.

These international and domestic legal writings outline a clear motif: voluntary consent that is free from force, coercion, and or duress. A societal vaccine passport which transforms liberties into privileges that are conditional on the acceptance of a medical procedure is a clear violation of both the notion of voluntary consent and the legal writings that defend it. Vaccine passports reserved the privilege of living an ordinary life, as a reward, to those who accepted the covid vaccine. Individuals who refused the vaccine were not only ostracized from ordinary life, but they were removed by police for "illegally" entering establishments open to the general public. It is an undeniable fact that vaccine passports cultivated an environment where individuals consented to a medical intervention under duress, coercion, and force.

The increase in vaccination uptake following vaccine passports proved in itself an element of duress. As intended, the covid vaccine passports compelled people to accept the vaccine after a prolonged period of refusal. This *giving in* moment was deliberately engineered as hesitant and reluctant individuals were pushed over the edge. Those who were reluctant, but eventually caved, reached their breaking point as a direct result of the draconian *consequences* that followed their refusal to "do their part for society." The coercive increase in vaccination uptake also hid the dark reality of those who remained adamant never to accept the covid vaccine. For it is these "rebellious" individuals that suffered the most mental anguish. The psychological torture of vaccine passports was twofold. Individuals were not only forced into physical and social isolation, but many who forged their vaccine certificates, to feed their families, lived under perpetual fear of being prosecuted. When lockdowns and vaccine passports plagued the west in 2020 and 2021, increase in suicide and depression were observed. Since then, many grieving parents have come out and blamed the government lockdowns and mandates for worsening their sons and daughters' wellbeing and in some cases contributing to their passing. The first publicized case of a person committing suicide in direct response to vaccine passports came from Germany on December 4, 2021.

In a house south of Berlin, police found five bodies: a father, mother, and their three children. The suicide note left behind told the story of a father who had killed his entire family, and then himself, after his employer had found out he had forged his wife's vaccine passport. The note explicitly mentioned that the father feared being imprisoned for disobeying the health authorities and feared social services would take away his children as a result. This story has a sense of eerie familiarity to the not-so-distant past, and for anyone who believed this case came unexpectedly need only inspect a little further.

On the third of December, a day prior to the incident, Germany enforced a seemingly indefinite and stringent lockdown on their unvaccinated population. This barred them from every establishment, except for groceries and pharmacies, and prohibited them from visiting more than two persons from another household. What further complicated matters was that the country, at the time, officially announced their intention to make covid vaccination compulsory. Germany was also notoriously militant with police "health" enforcement. A few weeks prior to the incident, a dozen people were arrested for allegedly selling forged vaccine passports. It was only a matter of time before the coercion to vaccinate, and the threat of imprisonment and social rejection, culminated in the deaths of individuals who would be alive today had they been treated like human beings rather than plague-ridden vermin.

Following the Berlin case, another incident gained media attention on April 27, 2022. In Cook County, Illinois, a lawsuit was filed by the family of a fifteen-year-old child who took his own life after being harassed and bullied relentlessly for his unvaccinated status. The child, however, was vaccinated and thus bullied on a rumour that spread. This was the end-product of vaccine passports; the cultivation of a society that vilifies the unvaccinated as "plague rats," "super-spreaders, "and "mutant factories." These two cases were the result of normalizing vaccine passports and consequently creating an inferior status of human beings. Those who advocated for vaccine passports evidently have blood on their hands, and they ought to be held accountable as accessories for the injustices they committed. In every war waged, there is collateral damage; no exception was made for the government's war on covid.

Individuals that were ostracized by vaccine passports, as a result of refusing a pharmaceutical injection, were more at risk of negative and fatal lifestyle outcomes. While these outcomes are more thoroughly discussed later, the inhumane consequences of vaccine passports hereto discussed highlight the ramifications of undermining medical consent. There is a reason that consent, and individual autonomy, is paramount to a free society and why it is that people have died to preserve such a right. It is wholly justified to label vaccine pass-ports as draconian, coercive, and one of the most dangerous govern-ment interventions in human history; an intervention that under-mined voluntary consent to medical procedures and threatened the core principles of what it means to be an autonomous human being.

HUMAN DIGNITY

Human dignity can be viewed as the intrinsic, inalienable right to be treated with basic respect in the eye of the law. That basic respect is predicated on being human and, as espoused by the United Nations Declaration of Human Rights, ought to be upheld irrespective of "race, colour, sex, language, religion, political or other opinion, natu-ral or social origin, property, birth, or other status."[7] Vaccine pass-ports were a government measure that barred an individual from essentially all public life on the grounds of their medical status and the biological contents of their immune system. On this basis alone, vaccine passports violated the enshrined right to human dignity and equal treatment under the law.

The right to a dignified life pertains to the fair opportunity to fulfill one's potential, or more specifically, the opportunity to attain the basic necessities. This right to human dignity is not to argue that people naturally deserve welfare or should be handed or owed it, but rather that no law nor government ought to restrict the oppor-tunity of man to attain their dignity. A dignified life is therefore merely one that is not treated unfairly or oppressed by the law. Gov-ernments that forced businesses to discriminate based on medical status, ostracizing patrons who did not meet vaccine passport requirements, wholeheartedly undermined this right. Vaccine passport unabashedly infringed on the dignity of the individual and their ability to attain a life of worth.

Let us briefly revisit the dystopian nature of the covid vaccination crusade as to highlight the extent that vaccine passports dehumanized the unvaccinated and consequently undermined the human dignity of the individual. Vaccine passports were implemented across society, deliberately intent on making life difficult for the unvaccinated individual. In the face of vaccine passports, the unvaccinated were largely unable to seek employment, education, and a sense of belonging. The peddlers of vaccine passports proudly championed these coercive consequences, for it was part of their greater design.

Among a list of confessions, French Health Minister Olivier Veran admitted that vaccine passports were a socially acceptable alternative to compulsory vaccination. In an interview with *Brut*, the French health minister believed that "blocking people from going to bars, restaurants and public places if they are not vaccinated is more efficient than slapping them with a 100 euro fine in the street."[8] Michael O'Leary, the Chief Executive Officer for Europe's largest airline group, Ryanair, made explicit his belief that governments should "make life very difficult" for people who refuse the covid vaccine and advocated that unvaccinated people "shouldn't be allowed in the hospital...shouldn't be allowed to fly...[and] shouldn't be allowed in the local supermarket."[9]

Echoing the dehumanizing sentiment of ostracizing the unvaccinated from public life, the *Toronto Star* was elated to report and endorse Quebec's Health Minister Christian Dube's following statement:

*"If they can't protect themselves, we will protect them against them-
selves… And we will make sure that they understand very clearly that
if they don't want to be vaccinated, they just stay home."*[10]

The premier of New Brunswick, Blaine Higgs, hours before he
reinstated a lockdown on his province in January of 2022, made public the coercive nature of his intentions. Higgs admitted that aggression was being imposed upon anyone who resisted the government's crusade, which he referred to as "the program." The premier
explicitly stated that he was "looking at all these things that would
make life more difficult for those that refuse to be part of the program and are able to do so."[11]

The following comments by Chicago Mayor Lori Lightfoot,
President of France Emmanuel Macron, and Prime Minister of Canada Justin Trudeau, remain the most Orwellian and thus worthy of
historical documentation. When she announced vaccine passports
to enter indoor spaces in Chicago, Lightfoot made the following despotic remark:

*"If you have been living vaccine-free, your time is up. If you wish to live
life with the ease to do things you love, you must be vaccinated. This
health order may pose an inconvenience to the unvaccinated, and in fact
it is inconvenient by design."*[12]

French President Macron, who was motivated to best the Chicago mayor as the most authoritarian government official, made this
statement two years into his own covid vaccine crusade:

*"I am not about pissing off the French people. But as for the non-vac-
cinated, I really want to 'piss them off. And we will continue to do this,
to the end. This is the strategy… we are putting pressure on the unvaccinated by limiting, as much as possible, their access to activities in*

social life... [the unvaccinated] are only a very small minority who are resisting. How do we reduce that minority? We reduce it... by pissing them off even more."[13]

The French president ended his tirade by insinuating the unvaccinated were non-citizens: "When my freedoms threaten those of others, I become someone irresponsible. Someone irresponsible is not a citizen."[14] The Canadian Prime Minister Justin Trudeau, notorious for demonizing the *unvaccinated*, had this to say to the Canadian people in one of his many divisive interviews:

"There is still a part of the population fiercely against [covid vaccination]. They don't believe in science or progress and are very often misogynistic and racist... They take up some space. This leads us, as a leader and as a country, to make a choice: do we tolerate these people?"[15]

I find myself wasting time trying to present the case that vaccine passports were deliberately intended to inflict suffering to disobedient citizens when political leaders have been so cooperative in admitting my point verbatim. In first writing this book I did not expect government officials to be so blatantly honest about their totalitarian decrees. Nevertheless, their transparency remains carved in history for the world to see.

Vaccine passports fostered a hostile and segregated environment that undermined the respect and dignity of the individual. The hostility perpetuated by vaccine passports was displayed throughout society, from medical professionals discerning whether unvaccinated patients should be given lesser priority in hospital care, to the American Dental Association council on ethics, bylaws, and judicial affairs encouraging dentists to decline and dismiss unvaccinated patients.

In the pseudo-private sector, large employers followed route with government dictate and instituted their own dehumanizing policies. One of the major airlines in the United States, Delta Air Lines, implemented a two-hundred-dollar monthly surcharge on their unvaccinated employees on November 1, 2021.[16] Given the airline's enthusiastic efforts to increase covid vaccination rates, it was unsurprising to find that the company had received 5.6 billion in federal subsides as part of a covid-19 relief program the year prior.[17] The CEO of Delta, Edward H. Bastian claimed the surcharge was necessary to address the financial risk the unvaccinated employees posed for the company. The airline dropped the surcharge, however, on April of 2022 because the CEO had changed his mind and decided covid-19 was a "seasonal virus."[18] It seems likely that the surcharge was merely a coercive and profitable scare tactic to boost vaccination uptake as part of a relentless crusade.

The grocery store giant, Kroger, similarly imposed a fifty-dollar monthly surcharge for all unvaccinated employees on January 1, 2022.[19] The company stated that the surcharge was meant to "encourage" workers to get the covid vaccine. After the year 2019, extorting money from someone with the intent of changing their behaviour became synonymous with "encouragement." Big businesses who enjoy preferential government treatment and subsidies were expectedly more than happy to punish those who refused a government-sponsored medical injection. In line with the quasi-fascist system of modern-day society, these employers were merely acting as loyal partners to the State.

In their inhumane pursuit to strip completely the dignity of the unvaccinated, governments proposed and enacted a litany of legislation ruthlessly targeting and punishing anyone who refused the covid vaccine. The state of Nevada approved a bill that would charge unvaccinated state workers a surcharge of up to fifty-five dollars per month. However, in March of 2022, months before the surcharge was set to be enforced, increased vaccination was cited as the reason for removing the bill.[20] The Austrian government, in November of 2021, announced a covid vaccine mandate for all residents over the age of eighteen.[21] The mandate was set to begin February of 2022. In a press conference announcing the mandate, Austria's Chancellor Karl Nehammer stated that "vaccination is the best guarantee for us to live together in freedom."[22] The Austrian mandate threatened routine police checks to confirm vaccination status and fines upwards of 3,600 euros a year for anyone unvaccinated.[23] Following unprecedented protests across the country, the government suspended the mandate in March and abolished the law "from its books" months later.[24]

In the beginning of 2022, the government of Greece notably fined unvaccinated citizens over the age of sixty. The country's vaccination uptake sufficiently increased in the following months, leading the government to suspend the mandate on April 15.[25] Italy updated its vaccine passport in February of 2022, making covid vaccination compulsory for anyone over the age of fifty.[26] A month following the update, the prime minister of Italy Mario Draghi hailed the "success of the vaccination campaign" as the reason he could "lift the remaining restrictions on people and companies."[27] Scaling back the vaccine passport did not save the Italian prime minister's declining popularity, however, as he resigned months later on July 21, 2022. While I hope the likes of Draghi will be remembered as the philanthropic tyrants they were, there will alas be some who shall see him as a martyr for the covid vaccine campaign – better referred to as a crusade.

As a consequence of requiring vaccination to partake in ordinary life, governments barred unemployment benefits for anyone who refused the covid vaccine. This prohibition affected anyone who was fired or unable to find employment as a result of the vaccine mandate. Alas, the government of Canada spearheaded this initiative. Justin Trudeau and his cabinet proudly believed that financially bankrupting and socially isolating its citizens would *encourage vaccine uptake*. Canada's Minister of Employment, Workforce Development and Disability Inclusion, Carla Qualtrough was ironically the person who announced that unvaccinated workers fired for their vaccine status would be ineligible for employment insurance.[28] In the spirit of Orwell, the minister of employment and inclusion turned out to be nothing of the sort.

New York City, proud of its pioneering and dystopian efforts to achieve a one-hundred percent vaccinated population, was the first of its kind to institute, on December 27, 2021, a vaccine passport mandate for the entirety of its private sector.[29] The mandate required that employers who employ "one or more workers" to show proof of covid vaccination, which included workers who were self-employed and or acted as sole proprietors.[30] Thus, citizens who employed a sole proprietor, such as a babysitter, were required within their own homes to demand proof of covid vaccination. The mayor of the city, Eric Adams, reiterated that the goal of the mandate was to "motiva[te] good behaviour."[31]

To further document the dystopian lengths that governments took to dehumanize the unvaccinated, Germany infamously required covid vaccination for the procedure of euthanasia.[32] The government's rationale was that euthanasia required "human closeness,"[33] which was considered a breeding ground for germ transmission and therefore outlawed to anyone not medically injected. When people referred to humans as social creatures, they must have exclusively meant vaccinated humans. In another display of inhumane government decree, Scotland mandated covid vaccination to access fertility treatment.[34] Its supporters evidently implicated that pregnancy is a privilege similarly reserved for the medically injected.

The prejudicial treatment from the government did not only dehumanize the unvaccinated, but it tore the family unit apart and deliberately so. Alongside financial hardships and social exclusion, the social consequences of vaccine passports on families were reprehensible. The establishment media, who were aware of the spiraling discord within families, blamed "antivaxxers," anti-government sentiment, and conspiracy theories. They blamed the individual and intentionally deflected from where the blame was rightfully meant to be. That is, on vaccine passports: the "public health" measure which instilled the notion that an individual was only worthy of an ordinary life as far as they accepted a government-provided pharmaceutical product.

In response to the hysteria surrounding hospital capacity and the fanatic desire to increase vaccination uptake, democrats in Illinois were one of the first in America to propose a bill to force unvaccinated hospital patients ailed with covid-19 to pay for their own medical bill.[35] This meant that a patient would be forced to disclose their vaccination status during treatment and penalized if their flu or cold symptoms turned out to be covid-19. The bill was expectedly withdrawn a few days after it was filed. Alas, democrats in Illinois were not alone in weaponizing healthcare to reduce the human worth of the unvaccinated.

The government of Singapore, who covered the costs of fully

vaccinated citizens, notably forced its unvaccinated citizens to cover their own health-care bills related to covid-19.[36] The Canadian province of Quebec, In January of 2022, announced a "health tax" on anyone who refused the covid vaccine. The premier of Quebec claimed that the unvaccinated "put a very important burden on our health-care network" and that a "majority of the population is asking that there be consequences."[37] Once vaccination in the population *sufficiently* increased following the announcement, Quebec rescinded the proposal. In America, a Rhode Island bill, introduced in March of 2022 by democrat senators, required the unvaccinated over the age of sixteen to pay a monthly civil penalty fine of fifty dollars and owe twice the amount of personal income tax.[38] The bill was similarly purported as a way for the state to compensate for the unvaccinated burden and which expectedly fell flat as several of the senators withdrew their names from the bill.

The rationale that kindled and laid justification for the weaponizing of the healthcare system against the unvaccinated was notably mantled, and argued, by covidians such as Canadian journalist, Diane Francis. Its advocates argued that certain groups who they deemed a burden on the system, i.e., the unvaccinated, ought to subsidize the costs of others while paying upfront for the very same service. Writing for the *Financial Times*, Diane espoused that the unvaccinated ailed with covid-19 should not "burden the vaccinated and other taxpayers with the medical costs [they] incur because of [their] own irresponsibility."[39] Despite its egregious irrationalities, this nationally televised argument increased public support for government policies targeting unvaccinated patients. Consequently, it is imperative for public record that the views of Diane Francis be unsparingly rebuked so that such a view may never justify government injustice again.

Diane Francis and advocates alike made their prejudice blatant when they referred to the unvaccinated as *burdening* the more privileged vaccinated taxpayers. The notion of forcing a select group of people to subsidize others while paying additional healthcare costs for "self-inflicted" injuries is both hypocritical and a slippery slope. Proponents of this prejudicial proposal did not, for example, advocate for individuals hospitalized for obesity-related ailments to similarly front their own hospital care. This double standard persisted despite the fact that obesity-related conditions contributed to the majority of covid hospitalized cases.[40]

It is evident that proponents such as Francis were merely vindictive towards those who refused to conform alongside them. Their contemptuousness is the reason they specifically demanded that a healthy unvaccinated patient, inflicted with covid-19, cover their own healthcare costs while forcing them to subsidize the costs of a vaccinated, obese patient hospitalized with covid. In other words, supporters of this discriminatory *healthcare reform policy* called on unvaccinated people to cover their own healthcare treatment for covid while paying the costs for others.

In their rhetoric there was never even mention of unvaccinated persons being exempt from paying into the taxpaid services they were barred from using. If the unvaccinated were to be denied or forced to pay additional fees to already subsidized services, including hospitals, airports, and other public spaces such as libraries and museums, then they ought to have been exempt from funding them for others. The privileged vaccinated who advocated for vaccine passports and mandates relished in their exclusivity and thus never cared to discuss such unfair conditions. In their mind, it was appropriate treatment towards a population they deemed as second class.

The advocacy for this vindictive healthcare policy, purported by individuals like Diane Francis, aided in garnering public support for healthcare-related taxes and surcharges that targeted the unvaccinated. With a majority that was told to be spiteful against the disobedient, governments across the world evidently threatened and, in some instances, implemented levies and fines on the unvaccinated. Their excuse was that the fine compensated the burden the unvaccinated placed on society. This egregious government overreach was not only outwardly despotic, but morally reprehensible and hypocritical. A tax or fine levied upon a person for their affiliation to an artificial and arbitrarily defined group, i.e., the unvaccinated, criminalizes and penalizes a person for their mere group identity. A healthy unvaccinated person, who never sought treatment or hospitalization for covid-19, was forced to pay for the supposed burden placed by other people in his or her apparent demographic. The unvaccinated were thus categorized, and penalized, for simply existing absence a government subsidized medical injection. This prejudice is not only dehumanizing but it eerily opens the door for justifying other forms of discrimination based upon group affiliation and a perceived "societal burden," i.e., a youth tax or, more specifically, a *black-youth tax*.

In America, black youth make up less than one quarter of the population while being responsible for more than half of juvenile violent crime arrest statistics in the United States, including over half of youth arrests for homicide and robbery.[41] One can argue that not only does this place a financial burden on both the healthcare and judicial system, but they pose a "statistical risk" to *society*. In the same way, an unvaccinated person, who makes up less than a quarter of the population in Canada, supposedly overrepresents covid-19 hospitalization admission statistics. Thus, as many proudly argued, not only are the unvaccinated a higher statistical risk to "public safety" but they similarly place a financial "burden" on healthcare services. The Canadian media was not shy to normalize this vitriol; *The Globe and Mail* headlined an article that read "Unvaccinated disproportionately risk safety of those vaccinated,"[42] while the *Toronto Star* similarly headlined their article, "Remaining unvaccinated increases risk to the vaccinated."[43] It is easy to replace the status of "unvaccinated" with any other identifying or group status, and redirect the danger of covid-19 to any other "societal threat," to observe its similarity to the dystopian past.

With that said, why stop at taxing and criminalizing the youth and the unvaccinated? Following such logic, the most frequent cause of hospitalizations in Canada is childbirth. It would therefore only be fair to implement a pregnancy tax to alleviate the burden females place on the healthcare system. The second most frequent hospitalization is pneumonia, which often requires hospitalization and ICU admission among seniors and persons with underlying health conditions. Consequently, where is the senior's tax for their burden on hospitals or the tax on the immune-comprised who may have developed immune deficiencies because of poor lifestyle choices. One might further ask where the alcohol, smoking, and sugar tax or fines are. How about a driving tax? After all, motor vehicle accidents place a toll on the healthcare system and pose comparatively higher safety risks. Considering covid hospitalization statistics, and to put an end to this never-ending slippery slope of lunacy, where was the obesity tax? As mentioned before, vaccination status was not the denominator for covid-19 severity, hospitalization, or death. Instead, covid severity was largely predicated on age and obesity among other underlying health conditions.

Akin to the legislation and policies targeting anyone who refused a covid vaccine, taxes and fines threatened upon the unvaccinated were mere scare tactics to increase vaccination. It had nothing to do with preventing hospital collapse or saving lives. Instead, the levies were meant to accompany the enforcement of vaccine passports as to punish more harshly the unvaccinated for refusing to "play their part." The proposed fines on the unvaccinated were also purported as a cathartic experience for the masses that were instructed to be vindictive towards the "anti-vaxxers." They were told that the unvaccinated were getting "what they deserved." In dystopian fashion, governments literally made the unvaccinated *pay the price* for their disobedience.

In another display of hypocrisy, these pro-discrimination advocates never once mentioned the "burden" that the vaccinated placed on other taxpaying groups, including those who declined the covid vaccine. Their silence was unwavering despite the rise of covid cases and hospitalizations among the vaccinated; the tens of millions in covid boosters that were government-purchased for the already double, triple, and quadruple vaccinated; and the mass covid testing that was coercively sold to the unvaccinated while subsidized free for the vaccinated. All these expenditures burdened the unvaccinated but alas the covidian zealots were shamelessly silent.

Vaccine passports, enforced by the iron hand of government, evidently cultivated an environment where covid vaccination proved to be the sole condition for an individual to be treated with dignity, respect, and bestowed the opportunity to attain a dignified life. In other words, covid vaccine passports compelled individuals to conform, risk bodily harm, and abandon their conscience all so they could have basic access to employment opportunities, health care

services, and the capacity for physical human connection and association. In this witnessed display of injustice, the democratic imperative to uphold human dignity – and maintain equal treatment under the law – proved nothing short of Orwellian.

CHARTERED RIGHTS

Alongside the violation of human dignity, vaccine passports infringe on the universally recognized constitutionally inscribed rights
to liberty, security, assembly, and conscience. In these transgressions
of sacrosanct proponents of a free society, vaccine passports ce-
mented their legacy as the most dehumanizing and egregious of
government interventions. A legacy that exposes the perversion of
democratic law and the fragility of liberties once believed to be inalienable. The analysis of the following rights is primarily referenced
in the context of Canadian law.

The Canadian charter upholds that "laws should not have a severe impact on people's right to life, liberty, or security of the person."[44]
The charter also "protects everyone against unreasonable laws that
could…harm their physical safety."[45] Vaccine passports functioned to
inhibit the individual from engaging in ordinary life unless medically
injected, which negatively impacted the liberty of the person in an
unprecedented fashion. The overt restrictions on liberty have been
thus far extensively documented. The harmful effects of vaccine
passports on the wellbeing of the individual have also been illuminated. In this section I therefore home in on its damaging impact to
the safety and security of the person – a reality that was ignored by
the covidian cult.

While touted as a health measure, vaccine passports posed a direct risk to the physical, mental, and social security of the individual. The segregation and societal exclusion ensued by government mandates that compelled vaccination negatively affected the wellbeing, both psychologically and financially, of any individual that refused to comply. The very act of mandating a medical intervention or pharmaceutical product also proved physically harmful. In order to abide by vaccine passports and partake in ordinary society, the individual was compelled to undergo the known and unknown risks associated with covid vaccination. The risks associated with the vaccine led the *few* to suffer its most fatal. Alas, the peddlers of covid vaccine passports considered it a worthy sacrifice. When vaccination uptake doubled in response to the use of vaccine passports, some were consequently harmed by the pharmaceutical injection. Given the nature of mandates, those negatively harmed by the covid vaccine complications were evidently coerced into hurting themselves. Vaccine passports therefore led some to consent to an injection under duress which, in some scenarios, also contributed to their unnatural death. Therein lies the indefensible government-sanctioned crime.

The societal exclusion that arose from vaccine passports particularly marginalized groups already prone to vulnerability. The homeless were one group that was significantly impacted by vaccine passports. The reasons being that the homeless are generally more in need for public assistance and were more likely to have not gotten the covid vaccine. Depending on their circumstances, some homeless folk may have also been unable to attain a vaccine passport or formally request an exemption from a medical or legal professional even if they so desired. The mandate to compel vaccination proof in all facets of society also exacerbated homelessness by leading to further unemployment, which was accompanied by limiting access to employment insurance and welfare assistance for anyone who was unemployed on account of their vaccination status. In other words, governments forced people onto the streets for refusing their sponsored pharmaceutical product. It truly seems the case that there are no *gods* more vindictive than government bureaucrats.

Despite the droves of unvaccinated employees terminated and suspended following the implementation of vaccine passports, the peddlers of covid vaccine passports erred on the side of denial. The self-righteous peddlers of vaccine passports were staunch in their belief that when pressured to the brink, everyone would vaccinate and be joyfully given back their freedoms. A part of them never intended to pull the trigger because they were confident no one would force their hand. Like Sauron – the antagonist from J.R.R. Tolkien's Lord of the Rings – who could not comprehend why anyone would refuse the power of the ring, the covidian zealots could not fathom why anyone would refuse such a divine gift and why anyone would fight back. This is partly the reason they were so angry with the unvaccinated. "Why are you making me do this," they must have thought. Governments were similarly unwavering in the face of their own authoritarianism, convinced that once the unvaccinated were forced onto the street, they would merely *give-in* and vaccinate. When governments are given reign to parent, the definition of *tough love* is redefined.

Minority groups that were similarly more likely to be unvaccinated, and historically prone to being marginalized, were black, Latino, and indigenous persons. On April 1, 2021, *Statistics Canada* reported that black and Latino Canadians were least willing to take the covid-19 vaccine.[46] One particular survey found that when sixty percent of eligible Canadians were vaccinated with at least one dose, not even half of black Canadians reported having been vaccinated.[47] On July 19, 2021, the Government of Canada reported just over half of indigenous folks (First Nations, Inuit, and territorial communities) reported being vaccinated with two doses.[48] Akin to the issues previously mentioned, indigenous groups are generally more likely to live in impoverished conditions and rely on public institutional assistance. The Canadian Poverty Institute estimates that nearly one in four indigenous people live in poverty.[49] While everyone who was unvaccinated met the wrath of segregation, aboriginals who were unvaccinated found themselves increasingly isolated.

Given the exacerbated impact on indigenous families and communities, vaccination uptake following the use of vaccine passports expectedly increased. On January 25, 2022, the Government of Canada reported that nearly ninety percent of the First Nations, Inuit, and territorial communities received their second vaccine dose.[50] The heightened socioeconomic vulnerability and dependency on government assistance within many aboriginal communities explains the "effectiveness" that vaccine passports had on the native population in Canada. It is difficult to believe that the sudden obedience observed by aboriginals, following nation-wide vaccine passports and mandates, was achieved without the iron hand of coercion. The sweeping mandate to compel vaccination proof led workplaces to fire or refuse to hire unvaccinated employees and universities to suspend and bar unvaccinated students and applicants. Whatever hardships fell generally on the unvaccinated population was exacerbated among aboriginals who already struggle under unfavorable socioeconomic conditions and opportunities.

The city of New York paid homage to antebellum America as its use of vaccine passports devolved the city into a "whites only" society.

On August 19, 2021, only twenty eight percent of young black New Yorkers, aged eighteen to forty-four were vaccinated. [51] What this means is that for a period of time, vaccine passports in New York City segregated from society seventy-two percent of young black individuals. To the racist's delight, it became unlikely to meet a black person in any establishment throughout the city. The city's vaccine passport also extended to children ages five to eleven, which exacerbated the public segregation of black youth and further hampered the socioeconomic advancements of stereotypically impoverished communities. Considering the mandate for businesses to compel vaccination, vaccine passports also led to the employment termination of black folks at disproportionate rates.

What blended comedy into this tragedy was that the segregation, instituted in the name of *public health*, arrived at the backdrop of an "anti-racist" government campaign that vowed to legislatively end "systemic racism" following a year long protest decrying racial police brutality in 2020. Ironically, the individuals who spearheaded initiatives to *incentivize* businesses to prohibit unvaccinated patrons were democrats and "liberal" idealogues that championed themselves as "anti-racist." These *progressive* incentives included rewarding pro-segregation employers with subsidies, threatening to impose restrictions, and outright closing defiant businesses down. The ultimatum the *anti-racists* and champions of inclusivity provided businesses was either to segregate or close shop. The slogan of "anti-racist" stamped on the uniform of any government bureaucrat proved perfectly Orwellian.

Governments sewing discord and strife among its subjects by propagating, normalizing, and incentivizing segregation has never been an uncommon phenomenon. The federal government of the

United States infamously subsidized contract builders, in the early-mid twentieth century, to create suburbs on the condition that the homes be sold to whites only. You need only replace the condition with "vaccinated only" to see the frightening parallel. In another previously mentioned example, the Louisiana's Separate Car Act of 1890 required passenger railways to separate black and white folks on its railway cars. In lieu of governments outright separating people based on vaccination status, which would be a step sideways from skin colour or ethnicity, the unvaccinated were altogether prohibited from entering passenger railways in many parts of the world. In Canada for example, unvaccinated travellers over the age of twelve were barred from planes and trains."[52] Various establishments and institutions, however, went the route of "separate but equal" as they separated the vaccinated from the unvaccinated in societal settings like classrooms, restaurants, and airport waiting lines.

My intention is not to conflate racial and medical segregation in any sort of competition, but merely to signify the gravity of the government-sanctioned segregation observed with the arrival of covid vaccine passports. Alas, the medical segregation towards the unvaccinated, and anyone who refused to participate in the charade of covid vaccine passports, measured up well to some of the most egregious State-enforced segregation policies in the last two hundred years. Once the hypnosis of the *pandemic* wanes with time, future generations will look back on the years between 2020-2022 with uneasiness. It will be a goldmine of cautionary tales and dystopian realities.

To delve briefly once more into the mirage of *democratic governance*, there is no one more skillful at *doublethink* than government bureaucrats. This is precisely the case because the essence of their position is to be the most attractive crowd pleasers and thus to present the most believable of illusions. A politician knows they cannot make everyone happy, and so they simply convince everyone that they are. In some ways, politicians of democracy are magicians, schooled in the art of illusion and allure. The most notable of State illusions is *persuading* the layman taxpayer, or voter, that their existence is both necessary and inevitable. All other subsequent illusions are secondary and act merely as complimentary. The government's *war on covid* was another one of its illusions, as were its other failed wars on drugs, poverty, and terrorism to name just a few. They seemingly have a war every generation because they need a reason to leech off each generation.

Peddlers of vaccine passports conceded that their creation disproportionately impacted the dignity, security, and wellbeing of various minorities. However, they deflected any responsibility or blame onto themselves by arguing that the unvaccinated phenomena within these minorities was simply due to a *lack of access*. In other words, the higher unvaccinated numbers were merely perceived to be an issue of infrastructure. Consistent with their progressive moral grandstanding, they implicitly assumed incompetence on behalf of blacks, Latinos, and aboriginals as though they were incapable or too poor to access a free and subsidized product or service. Their belief was that once they handed them the covid vaccines at the door, the uneducated unvaccinated would accept it uniformly like obedient slaves. The self-righteous, condescending, and dishonest nature of those who peddled vaccine passports was displayed for the world to see and will be remembered for time immemorial.

The next sacrosanct chartered principle that vaccine passports violate is the right to peaceful assembly. The freedom of assembly is famously championed in most western democracies, and the Canadian charter specifically outlines each "person's right to gather with others and express ideas."[53] This freedom however, and the entirety of the Canadian charter, was evidently nullified in the face of vaccine passports, which denied the unvaccinated the freedom to gather and coexist with other humans. This prohibition on association extended into the heart of Canadian parliament.

In November of 2021, The House of Commons Speaker, Anthony Rota, required all members of parliament to be fully vaccinated against covid-19.[54] On June 3, 2022, Saskatchewan MP Cathay Wagnall was forcefully removed from Parliament for violating the vaccine mandate.[55] Humorously, knowledge of Wagnall's vaccination status at the time of her forceful eviction was unknown. The Saskatchewan MP was thus simply removed for refusing to disclose whether she had accepted the government's approved list of injections. In a motif that permeated vaccine passports, individuals were punished not for specifically being unvaccinated but rather for staying silent and refusing to orally pledge allegiance.

Not only did covid vaccine passports prohibit individuals from peacefully assembling absent a medical injection, but elected unvaccinated officials were unable to congregate and fulfill their *democratic duty* as "public servants." Parliament members who refused the covid vaccine were allowed to participate virtually, which justified the unprecedented mandate. It is a dystopian slope, however, to utilize technological or corporate applications as justification for constitutional violations. Microsoft computers and iPhones being utilized as an excuse to breach the constitution is rather fitting for the parody that is our *democratically free society.*

Vaccine passports exclusively *grant* vaccinated individuals the ability to exercise the right of peaceful assembly. This makes the constitutional right to assembly solely conditional on the acceptance of a pharmaceutical product, being in this case a vaccine. If monarchs and kings of the past mandated medical procedures and pharmaceutical injections as a condition to congregate and assemble, one can only imagine the world we would live in today. The war on covid displayed a level of dictatorial might that would have ignited a litany of revolutions if it were attempted in centuries past. Luckily for the governments of the twenty-first century, they enacted their tyranny with the most docile and subservient of populations.

The most egregious violation of the covid vaccine passports pertained to the conscientious right of the individual. A right that I consider to be the most fundamental proponent of liberty. Conscience – being our moral sense and the psychological lens for which we view the world – is an integral part of consciousness itself and thus an inseparable component of our human existence. In many ways, our moral compass both shapes and embodies who we are as human beings. The most fundamental of human liberties is alas ill-defined among all "free democratic societies." Nevertheless, as it pertains to conscience, the Supreme Court of Canada ruled the following in 2015:

> *"The pursuit of the ideal of a free democratic society requires the state to encourage everyone to participate freely in public life regardless of their beliefs...[and to preserve] a neutral public space free from coercion, pressure, and judgement...The state's duty to protect everyone's freedom of conscience and religion means that it may not use its powers in such a way as to promote the participation of certain believers or non-believers in public life to the detriment of others."*[56]

The legal literature in Canada also dictates that "freedom of conscience is aimed more broadly at protecting views based on strongly held moral ideas of right and wrong."[57] This imperative of state neutrality and free participation as it involves the conscience of the individual is universally present, albeit dubiously, in most western democracies. It is easy to argue that consent for and against covid vaccination, and broadly any medical procedure, is based upon some belief or moral conviction. All of our decisions are invariably dictated by our conscience or moral frame of reference. A person unable to consent is, for example, generally perceived to lack the cognitive ability to formulate a belief or conviction relating to the situation.

An individual that utilized their right and refused to consent to the covid vaccination thus made a moral judgment that they were uncomfortable with a particular set of risks associated with a pharmaceutical product. They may have also held the conviction to gain natural immunity instead. These reasons, however, were deemed unacceptable by the State and thus the dissenters were both segregated and punished for their *blasphemous* existence. How intolerable, indeed, is the audacity of government to presume itself rightful to dictate the freedoms to be exercised by humanity. This intolerance is heightened when such a freedom to be denied involves existing in the world absent a pharmaceutical injection.

I have abstained from discussing freedom of religion on the basis that it is, or ought to be, related to conscience. Most vaccine passports and vaccine mandates, albeit not all, made some room for religious exemption. No such exemption existed for someone who wanted to merely refuse the covid vaccination for other personal, non-religious reasons. This discrepancy is rooted in the fact that most constitutions explicitly recognize freedom of religion, at least more so in comparison to conscience. This is also why immunization regiments often make room for religious objections without nearly as much penalty or scorn. A peculiarity in our "free democratic society" is that beliefs rooted in religion or divinity are often better protected and respected than beliefs of a secular nature. Whether or not a person's conscience lies in either religious, secular, or other rationale need not matter for the conscience of an agentic human adult ought to be indiscriminately upheld and respected. This necessity is paramount when it pertains to one's own body and biological contents.

The likely reason that conscience is poorly protected and ignored in the free democratic west relates to both the preservation of government coercion and the persecution of "victimless crimes." The most favored of these coercive demands relates to taxation and the crime of its evasion. In a world that respects the choice and self-determination of conscious and sentient adults, there would no longer be room for government officials to force their dictate on others. Alas, the modern democratic State has bestowed authority onto itself to dictate the conscience of its citizenry and thus the persecution of victimless crimes, or *dissident behaviour*.

The power of governments to punish victimless acts, or human behaviour where no one is aggressed upon, is what lays the foundation for all government injustice, including vaccine passports. A government that truly upholds the conscience of its citizens would be morally incapable of criminalizing people for their victimless behaviour. Briefly, a victimless crime constitutes an action that does not aggress upon another but is nonetheless legally punished for personal or subjective moral preferences. These crimes are decided by governments on a whim and are continually amended according to the predilections of the present rulers. Individuals fined for refusing the covid vaccine, and therefore a pharmaceutical product, were essentially prosecuted for a victimless act.

To protect the conscience of the individual, and their right to self-determination, as far as it does not aggress upon the body or property of another, leads to a moral re-examination of taxation. In the eye of government, this would be the most dangerous consequence of respecting conscience and the liberty for persons to live their life as they choose. Modern taxation is, briefly, a levy coercively imposed onto the citizens by its governments. Taxation is rightfully perceived as a form of extortion considering the individual has their possessions confiscated from them. Despite this clear moral violation, there is no way to object to it. The tax objector's conscience is rational and factual but alas their concerns are futile. No one can object to taxation because the conscience of such an objection is not recognized nor protected. For the government to maintain its economic, political, and social power – and consequently preserve the present hegemony – the tax objector's conscience must be denied at all costs.

The conversation of taxation is important in any discussion of government injustice, including vaccine passports, because the existence of taxation – which lies at the heart of government itself – gives legitimacy for all subsequent government violations. Compulsory taxation confiscates the fruits of one's bodily labour and thus hinders the very notion of self-ownership. With the existence of taxation, any argument for bodily autonomy is inherently hampered or diminished. If one cannot refuse a cheque demanded by the State, what rationale would enable them to refuse a pharmaceutical injection demanded by that same government entity? The justification for taxation also unsurprisingly runs parallel to the justification for compulsory vaccination, or vaccine passports, being that it is *an obligation to society*. Alongside taxation, the same can be observed with conscription – which is the government-sanctioned confiscation of a person's bodily service. In a nation that enables government the right to conscript people, predicated on a presumed "duty to society," there is truly little ground to argue for bodily autonomy or anything of the sort.

When it comes to the edict of government, the conscience of its citizenry means truly little. The State defines, dictates, and assumes sole responsibility in *protecting* the individual and consequently the fabric of their existence. Governments assume this philanthropic responsibility deceptively as to monopolize the power to impose upon its citizens at will, mandate as its sees fit, and grant exemptions preferentially to the lifestyles it deems acceptable or politically beneficial. In his essay *Willing Slaves of the Welfare State*, the late C.S. Lewis eloquently articulated the suffocating grasp that governments have been culminating over the everyday life of every man, woman, and child:

> *"The modern State exists not to protect our rights but to do us good or make us good...hence the new name 'leaders' for those who were once 'rulers'. We are less their subjects than their wards, pupils, or domestic animals. There is nothing left of which we can say to them, 'Mind your own business.' Our whole lives are their business."*[58]

This cultivation of government power bloomed during the war on covid, as "leaders" turned into deities and humans into *livestock*, stripped of their individuality for the security of the hive. The liberty to live freely as dictated by one's conscience, particularly in respect to what individuals accept into their bodies, will always be threatened by the existence of vaccine passports. There is no hope for liberty while they exist. The repercussions of such a liberty to be lost would evidently be devastating. *Cogito, ergo sum* – I think therefore I am. Without the liberty of conscience and the liberty to think as we are, our existence will never truly be our own.

The Law

While I have dedicated time to defend constitutional liberties, there seems to be something very wrong with relying upon a sole entity to ensure the preservation of natural rights. And if such an entity has enabled government levies, the coercive payment and acceptance of pharmaceutical products, and the closing down of businesses who refused to segregate its patrons, then its purpose is truly corrupted beyond repair. With every government atrocity that transpires, constitutions and charters admit themselves as a vehicle to justify and legalize oppression. It is alas the case that individual freedoms and liberties being tempered and tampered by a system of *democracy* – i.e., groups of power-hungry officials – is in fact part of the problem. It is the sole force that birthed the tyrannical war on covid and the authoritarian, philanthropic governance of the last century.

Alas, so long as we continue to give a centralized and omnipotent entity the right to dictate and define our liberties, the longer we shall be forever chained on a whim. The realization that we do not live in a free society, but rather are coercively governed by people who pretend to speak on behalf of the *greater will*, has never been clearer than it is today. If there is to be any consolation to the dreadful birth of vaccine passports, it is that more people have awakened to the illusion of democratic governance. May the rise of tyranny, cloaked in the philanthropic promise of security, rebirth the view of liberty as it once was and has always been – *freedom from the government.*

Part IV:
Constitutionality

Chapter 8

THE OAKES TEST:

A SUMMARY

*Everything a government pleases to do will, of course, be deter-
mined to be constitutional, if the government itself be permitted to
determine the question of the constitutionality of its own acts.
Those who are capable of tyranny, are capable of perjury to sus-
tain it.*

Lysander Spooner[1]

As you might have come to expect, I take no pride in using
government concocted tools and tests to assess whether
government itself acted in wrongdoing. Nevertheless, this
chapter demonstrates the failure of vaccine passports to pass a constitutional assessment known as the Oakes Test. In the process of reiter-
ating its failure, the dehumanizing and invasive reality of vaccine
passports is summarized. The constitutional test, created by the Supreme Court of Canada in 1986, examines section 1 of the *Charter of
Rights and Freedoms*, better known as the "reasonable limits clause."
This section states that rights are "subject only to such reasonable
limits...as can be demonstrably justified in a free and democratic society."[2] This clause legally allows government to limit chartered
rights and thus make no right inalienable. In plain language, the test

asserts whether an infringement on an individual's-chartered right is warranted, reasonable, and justified. While I am of the mind that tyranny is never warranted, reasonable, or justified, the crux of our democracy lies in the array of clauses that enable government the right to infringe upon natural rights and liberties whenever *public interest* is supposedly threatened. If there is one thing that this book has made apparent, however, it is that the charter's association of "free" and "democratic" is nothing short of Orwellian.

The relevant part of the Oakes test is compartmentalized into three sections: the first assesses whether the charter's infringement is arbitrary or illogical in connection to the law's purpose. The law, in this scenario, is domestic or societal covid vaccine passports. The government-enforced vaccine passports, which exclusively bestowed freedoms onto the vaccinated, were instituted under the premise of reducing transmission. However, this intention was innately flawed and arbitrary considering the fact that vaccinated people contracted and spread covid-19.

The Government of Canada has readily acknowledged that "vaccinated people can still get infected if exposed…[which] means that even with high vaccine effectiveness, some vaccinated people will get sick, be hospitalized, or die."[3] The Canadian government even admitted that, in response to high vaccination rates, "there will naturally be more cases among vaccinated people than among un-vaccinated people."[4] The trend of higher transmission among the vac-cinated was similarly observed in the United States and notably highlighted by a *Washington Post* headline that read: "A growing per-centage of Americans dying from covid-19 are vaccinated."[5] In the face of these admissions, uttered by its own government handlers, the premise of vaccine passports to prevent transmission falls further by the wayside. Individuals that had the covid vaccine were transmitting covid-19 the moment vaccine passports were instituted, and they continued to do so throughout 2022. The mandate thus fabricated an arbitrary privilege upon one group of people – the vaccinated – who were exclusively allowed to spread covid in certain indoor and outdoor spaces. Given the dystopian reality that vaccine passports cultivated, its existence and enforcement ought to be deemed discriminatory, arbitrary, and illogical.

The next section of the test assesses whether the law infringement is minimal, impairs the chartered right "as little as possible," and or is "within a range of reasonably supportable alternatives." For the sake of the test, we shall home in on Ontario's vaccine passport which only recognized vaccination and excluded both alternatives of natural immunity and negative tests. The first obvious violation is thus the failure to provide alternatives to a person refusing the covid vaccine. The denial of entry absent proof of pharmaceutical injection into societal spaces such as museums, theatres, weddings, restaurants, concerts, college lecture halls, libraries, and hospitals when entering as a visitor did not impair "as little as possible" the rights of the individual to freely partake in ordinary society.

Physical distancing and mask mandates may comparatively be more likely of meeting the threshold of impairing "as little as possible" the rights of the individual. After all, individuals subjected to such requirements are still able to enter establishments, entertain services, and congregate with others granted they mantle a temporary piece of cloth and or arbitrarily keep a physical distance. Bestowing onto government the right to force citizens to cover their faces and maintain a specified distance whilst interacting, however, warrants its own Orwellian slope. The mask and distancing mandates also appeared, unsurprisingly, as ineffective as vaccine passports to *reduce transmission.*

The more demanding and invasive a restriction or requirement is the more likely it is to impair, beyond a *reasonable* limit, the individual's natural rights – which are the liberties that all humans are born with. In comparison to the mandates that compelled mask-wearing and physical distancing, the mandate to vaccinate was the most extreme. In other words, the most demanding and invasive government mandate during the war on covid was unequivocally domestic vaccine passports. The government measure coerced an individual to express consent to a medical injection as the only means to enter societal spaces, congregate in assembly with other human beings, and maintain employment to feed their families.

If there is ever a "public health measure" that extends to the extreme, it ought to be vaccine passports – for if vaccine passports do not violate the "democratic" constitution, no public health measure ever will. It is difficult to brainstorm a measure more damning than vaccine passports without blatantly crossing over into totalitarianism. No other government intervention, cloaked in philanthropic intentions, has ever been more invasive and demanding in the history of mankind. "If not vaccine passports, then what"? I ask. Those who were not determined to die on the hill opposing compulsory covid vaccination and vaccine passports are unlikely to stand on any hill at all. If you did not stand against the government forcing upon you a pharmaceutical injection, on the threat of societal exclusion and punitive fines, then what is there left to stand for?

A vaccine passport is a dystopian requirement that on its face nullifies basic notions of liberty and, more covertly, implicates vaccination and the acceptance of medical procedures as constitutional conditions to exercise supposedly inalienable liberties. Akin to chickens being vaccinated before being allowed to interact with other livestock, so too would humans find themselves incapable of basic interaction unless first injected. The advocates of vaccine passports are unabashed in their treatment of humans as domesticated livestock to be subjected to the whims of bureaucratic and academic shepherds.

The last section of the Oakes Test examines proportionate effects. In other words, whether the infringement on the individual is a price too high to pay in relation to the advancements of the law's purpose. Immediately it is apparent, that there were no advancements; vaccine passports accomplished absolutely nothing. To reiterate the failure of vaccine passports throughout the world, let us revisit the "advancements" of vaccine passports and see how the measure faired against the test of proportionality.

"ADVANCEMENTS"

On February 1, 2022, Finland's Minister of Justice Anna-Maja Henriksson, who had once claimed vaccine passports were a measure intended to stop virus spread, could no longer justify its use:

> *"The coronavirus passport limits the basic rights of those people who haven't got vaccinated, obtained a negative result, or had the disease. The Coronavirus or vaccination passport isn't well suited for use in these circumstances because its necessity and proportionality is difficult to justify right now."*[6]

Judicial systems in the west all have their own constitutional assessment to gauge proportionality because all democracies enable government-sanctioned infringements on liberty. In the year 2022, the government of Finland decided vaccine passports could no longer be rationalized. What Finland's minister failed to admit, however, was that vaccine passports were never warranted in the first place. Despite whatever intention were behind its use, a mandate to compel businesses to segregate the unvaccinated was never going to prevent the transmission of one single germ.

The "advancements," or failures of vaccine passports, were easily predicted from the beginning. Following Austria's abolition of its compulsory vaccine mandate on June 23, 2022, the country's Health Minister Johannes Rauch admitted that "no one is getting vaccinated because of the compulsory vaccination."[7] Alas, these admissions from the leading crusaders were too little too late – for the injustice had already been committed. Such an unprecedented tool, which arbitrarily segregated individuals by their *medical injection* status, was merely a project of coercion and aggression. The only fruits to bear from its branches were seemingly half-empty apologies and admissions of colossal failure.

To further document the abysmal efficacy of vaccine passports, let us briefly turn to the Canadian provinces of Quebec and Ontario; the countries of Israel, New Zealand, Iceland, Germany, Portugal, and Australia; and the cities of Hong Kong and New York. The province of Quebec was one of the first to authorize emergency powers and call for a lockdown on March 15, 2020. They were also the first in Canada to institute vaccine passports in September of 2021. What did Quebec, however, have to show for all their progressive and bold government measures? On January 1, 2022, Quebec reported 17,122 new covid-19 cases which totaled a new record.[8] In that same week, the province reinstated a two-week lockdown and proposed

174

a tax on the unvaccinated. To provide some perspective, the province reported 656 covid cases the day the government instituted vaccine passports.[9]

Quebec was not an isolated case exemplifying the utter failure of vaccine passports and related mandates in Canada. The province of Ontario, famous for one of the strictest vaccine passports and longest lockdowns in the world, reached record covid transmission into the year 2022. On January 1, 2022, Ontario similarly recorded a record high of 18,445 new covid-19 cases.[10] During that time, Ontario enacted its own three-week lockdown which closed, once again, restaurants, gyms, and various indoor and outdoor gathering spaces. In a failed spectacle, Ontario instituted their vaccine passport on September 22, 2021, when the province reported only 463 new covid cases.[11] Both Quebec and Ontario reported record breaking covid transmission at the heel of more than eighty percent of their populations vaccinated, which was achieved through government coercion.

Deflecting responsibility from the inefficacy of vaccine passports, Justin Trudeau blamed the unvaccinated for the reinstated lockdowns around the country. In one of his many dystopian remarks, the Canadian prime minister stated that "when people see that we are in lockdowns or serious public health restrictions right now because of the risk posed to all of us by the unvaccinated…people get angry."[12] The president of the United States, Joe Biden, eerily mirrored Trudeau's sentiment when he reassured Americans "who have gotten vaccinated," that he understood their "anger at those who haven't gotten vaccinated."[13] The *Toronto Star*, infamously known as the Canadian media outlet that most fervently vilified the unvaccinated, made the following dystopian remark on January 9, 2022:

"Time to raise the price for those who still won't get vaxxed…the respon- sible majority of citizens are fed up with their locked-down ears with the anti-vax tail wagging the dog…Reason hasn't worked. Statistics haven't worked. Pleading, begging scolding and shaming haven't worked…Those refusing to be vaccinated against COVID-19 are doing great harm to the majority of responsible citizens."[14]

This divisive and hateful rhetoric was propagated by govern- ment media at a time when vaccine passports segregated millions of unvaccinated individuals from every aspect of ordinary life. In Feb- ruary of 2022, anyone in Canada who was unvaccinated could not legally enter, as previously mentioned, a litany of spaces including restaurants, gyms, movie theatres, and museums. The unvaccinated could not board commercial flights and passenger trains and were barred from enrolment in most public universities. They were also prohibited from entering hospitals as visitors and thus could not ac- company sick family members. Much of these restrictions continued into the summer of 2022. In Quebec, they were not even legally al- lowed to enter the grocery aisle in Walmart and Costco nor patron government-owned liquor and marijuana stores. The unvaccinated were also threatened with an "anti-vax tax" which was later with- drawn by Quebec's Premier Francois Legault after he came to the profound realization that the tax "divide[d] Quebecers."[15]

To reiterate, one of the most criminal and dehumanizing conse- quences of vaccine passports pertained to the fact that unvaccinated citizens were barred from using services their tax money was simul- taneously funding. Fanning the flames of such absurdity, unvac- cinated persons in Canada also forfeited their hard-earned money to a federal and provincial institution that discriminately refused to hire them. While once hailed as essential to the preservation of society, hundreds of unvaccinated firefighters, health-care workers, and police officers in Canada were forced on unpaid leave following the arrival of vaccine passports.

The vaccine passports implemented nationally in Canada made the unvaccinated student and workforce population both non-existent and entirely virtual. To most suburban and city-dwelling Canadians, the unvaccinated person did not exist in their reality. They did not walk or sit among them and if they did, it was done so illegally. The average vaccinated Canadian perceived anyone who was unvaccinated as either dead in hospital or an imminent danger to the public. Very few groups in history have been so harshly demonized for doing nothing but existing in their own bodies.

In spite of all the restrictions that imprisoned the disobedient, government officials and their funded mouthpieces persistently demonized, harassed, and blamed the unvaccinated. They scapegoated a group of people for every ill that befell society and stoked fear that pitted neighbours against one another. A professor at the University of Toronto, Dr. Kerry Bowman, reflecting on the climate of Canadian society in 2022, believed that "you could practically propose going after the unvaccinated with pitchforks and torches and you'd get support for that."[16] It was either governments and their funded media that tore apart Canadian society or the truth simply reared its ugly head. The truth that Canada is not the polite, inclusive, and free country it has pretended itself to be.

Before I discuss the other countries and cities that exemplified the failure of vaccine passports, it is important to briefly address the notion, popularized by many including the *Toronto Star*, that equated being a responsible citizen with being vaccinated. The association of responsibility and preferred medical status echo that of supremacy rhetoric. This rhetoric was transparent in its belief that someone who accepted the covid vaccine was more responsible and more competent than their unvaccinated counterpart. The favoritism towards anyone who accepted the covid vaccine was a judgment made solely on state allegiance and a particular biological characteristic. That explains the reason individuals with natural immunity, during the covid vaccine crusade, were demonized akin to the unvaccinated.

Despite the vaccinated person and the individual with natural immunity both having some form of antibodies and thus protection to covid-19, the vaccinated person was deemed the responsible and competent one because they had the preferred biological makeup i.e., vaccinated antibodies. The favoured individual was the one that "did their part" and had the biology and government documentation to prove it. The privileges and rewards granted exclusively to anyone who was vaccinated created a social climate ripe for vaccine supremacy. The vaccinated were free to dine inside as they watched their inferiors forced to eat in their cars or on the sidewalk. It was therefore unsurprising that such rhetoric was popular among the impressionable masses during the height of vaccine passports.

Most countries that coerced their populace to reach record high vaccination rates through vaccine passports were rewarded with unprecedented covid transmission. The war they waged on covid was expectedly a resounding failure. With the arrival of the covid vaccines, Israel prided themselves on pioneering the covid vaccination crusade. On July 11, 2021, an Israeli production company even aired a documentary called "Vaxxed Nation," which praised Israel as a "world leader at vaccinating its population."[17] Israel was one of the first countries to implement covid vaccine passports for everyday life; the first to update the definition of "fully vaccinated" to include boosters; and one of the first to offer a fourth covid vaccine dose or a second booster.

In the face of their pioneering efforts, the "Vaxxed Nation" reached record levels of covid transmission months following their supposed success. On January 5, 2022, Israel's health ministry announced the country was experiencing "nearly 12,000 new coronavirus cases" which constituted "the largest daily rise in infections since the beginning of the pandemic nearly two years ago."[18] The country did see a reduction in covid cases in March akin to the rest of the world, however it was no thanks to vaccine passports. Instead, one could have merely thanked the changing of seasons and the passing of time.

The New York Times notably declared that New Zealand was undergoing a "Covid Reckoning" as the country reached a covid case count record of 23,194 on March 3, 2022.[19] Ironically, the country was once believed "Covid-19 free"[20] and hailed for having "defeated the virus."[21] New Zealand was one of the first *success stories* which resulted in the country being used as precedent to justify lockdowns, mandates, and passports around the world. The country's failure was particularly tragic as it accompanied immeasurable economic and psychological damage bequeathed by their prime minister, and pioneer of vaccine passports and lockdowns, Jacinda Arden. The prime minister infamously boasted that vaccine passports were creating "two different classes" and remarked that vaccine passports were not only beneficial to "drive up vaccines" but to increase "confidence" for those who have been vaccinated and "want to know they're around other vaccinated people."[22]

The covid vaccination crusade in Germany similarly turned out to be a totalitarian embarrassment. Following one of the harshest government mandates and vaccine passports, the country experienced a record high of reported coronavirus infections on March 10, of 2022, totaling 262,752 daily cases.[23] This record was achieved at the backdrop of German chancellor Olaf Scholz's emphatic assertion, on the eve of 2022, that covid vaccines were "our way out of the pandemic."[24] *The Washington Post* published a headline on September 30, 2021, that read "Portugal has nearly run out of people to vaccinate," and asked "what comes next?"[25] Two months following its publication, Portugal introduced vaccine passports because their Prime Minister António Costa felt the country was "not [doing] as well" as he had wanted.[26] Considering that irony is the most popular motif permeating the nature and use of vaccine passports, what came next was wholly expected. On June 6, 2022, the local newspaper *Portugal Resident* reported that "Portugal remains the European Union country with the largest number of new cases of infection by SARS-CoV 2 per million inhabitants…and the second in the world in this indicator."[27]

The country that arguably displayed the most aggressive police-state in human history between 2020-2022, for the "health" of its citizens, was Australia. As a result of some of the strictest vaccine passports and lockdowns in the world, the vaccinated population in Australia reached over ninety percent. *The Washington Post* even praised the country and its government, publishing a headline in November of 2020 that read "Australia has almost eliminated the coronavirus by putting faith in science."[28] Alas, the country experienced record covid transmission in 2022 as its Northern Territories declared a lockdown exclusively for the unvaccinated. While lockdowns that solely targeted the unvaccinated were received with a few gasps even from the mainstream masses, they were no different to the vaccine passports implemented in places like Canada.

The Oakes Test

The city of Hong Kong, once hailed as the success story of mask-wearing and government intervention towards covid-19, reported a record level of new coronavirus infections totaling 56,827 on March 3, 2022.[29] Vaccine passports, mask mandates, and a population near eighty percent double vaccinated proved fruitless even for the poster child of *public health tyranny*. Despite the failures of Hong Kong, the city of New York ranks as the number one city to exemplify the embarrassing failure of vaccine passports. The metropolitan city was the first in America to implement one of the strictest vaccine passports in the world as well as one of the harshest vaccine mandates. It was therefore ironic that on January 8, 2022, the city reported a record breaking 47,591 new covid-19 cases.[30] When New York began enforcing its vaccine passport on September 13, 2021, the city recorded only a seven-day average of 1,868 covid cases.[31]

One could even make the argument that vaccine passports contributed to the fluctuating highs of covid transmission. After all, covid transmission universally spiked in countries and cities that implemented vaccine passports. There is no evidence indicating that absent vaccine passports, these regions would have fared worse. On the contrary, the data points in the opposite direction.

The American states of Florida and Texas were one of the two most populated regions that abstained from using vaccine passports. In fact, they both notably prohibited businesses from mandating covid vaccination. According to *The New York Times*, the daily average for covid cases on January 7, 2022 – which was the week that covid transmission peaked around the world – was 56,682 in Florida, 53,266 in Texas, and 70,426 in New York.[32] In the first week of 2022, the four American states that reported the most covid cases per capita were Rhode Island, New York, New Jersey, and Massachusetts.[33]

All four states, including New York, had vaccination rates above the national average and implemented vaccine passports. Six of the ten states with the fewest covid cases per capita in the same week had vaccination rates lower than the national average and eight of the states abstained from various covid-related government restrictions.[34] The state of Idaho, which reported the lowest number of covid cases per-capita, had the lowest vaccination rate in the country and banned vaccine passports entirely.

Let us take this comparison abroad to the country known for the most brutal covid lockdowns, mandates, and passports. On January 13, 2022, Australia recorded a daily average of 109,215 covid-19 cases, which was almost more than the cases in Florida (63,892) and Texas (56,256) combined.[35] The failure of Australia's crusade against covid was further exemplified by the fact that their population was over ninety percent vaccinated, which was thirty percent more than the populations of Florida and Texas. Regions that coercively compelled their population to vaccinate, such as Australia and New York, evidently experienced either the same or higher covid transmission compared to similarly populated metropolitan regions that did not segregate the unvaccinated. This basic observation, despite whatever nuance can be found, unequivocally illuminates the debacle of vaccine passports.

The hypothesis that vaccine passports increased covid-19 transmission, while admittedly lacks explicit causational proof, is as valid an argument as the notion that vaccine passports reduced covid transmission. The latter, arguably, exists even less evidence for. Vaccine passports were correlated towards increased covid transmission alongside a plethora of other mental, financial, and social detriments. The more palpable conclusion, however, is that vaccine mandates and passports, in relation to covid transmission, simply proved arbitrary and meaningless.

The layman supporter of vaccine passports holds stubbornly onto the belief that their creation reduced transmission despite admissions from their own governments to the contrary. As documented throughout the book and admitted to by its own handlers, the only "effectiveness" of vaccine passports pertained to coercively increasing vaccination uptake. Even to this purported objective, many governments demonstrably lamented the fact that vaccine mandates were not sufficiently increasing vaccination uptake in their respective populations. Thus, even among their own wicked standards, vaccine passports were an utter failure. This failure, however, does not acquit them of the crime they have committed.

To pressure someone, through social or financial punishment, to accept a medical injection that carries even the slightest risk of bodily harm, ought to be considered a crime against humanity. To have even insisted that another individual take the risks of blood clotting and heart inflammation, two prominent risks associated with covid vaccines, as the only means to congregate with others or earn a living to feed one's family is truly unconscionable. This grave injustice is made worse when you consider that heart inflammation and deep vein thrombosis, which is a type of blood clotting most reported following covid vaccination, predispose the individual to an increased risk of heart attacks. As illustrated throughout the book, the physical, financial, social, and mental hardships that were experienced by those who refused to accept the covid vaccine or participate in the vaccine passport program were prices too high to pay for whatever fictional "advancements" came with vaccine passports.

Covid vaccine passports demonstrably violated the Oakes Test.

As mentioned before, however, we need not a government test to label vaccine passports as morally and constitutionally abhorrent. What is wrong is wrong, no matter if it is sanctioned by democratic men in government attire. With that said, I hope this brief discussion of the law as it pertains to fundamental moral principles further illuminates the dehumanizing nature and dystopian implications of vaccine passports.

It is to be cautioned, that if freedom passports judged upon the willingness to accept a medical or pharmaceutical injection are not deemed as constitutional violations, then not only have we buried the very notion of a constitution, but we have created the most dangerous precedent known to man. A precedent that will come to haunt future generations, complicating liberty long after we, who stand here today, are gone. *Philanthropic tyranny*, which has become a signature of twenty-first century democratic governance, comes first with a smile and gentle hand and thus we must discern its smirk so as to not let it grab onto our necks.

Part V:

Epilogue

Chapter 9

SEEDS OF HOPE

The more a man becomes aware, through reflection, of his servile condition, the more indignant he becomes, the more the...spirit of freedom, determination, and action waxes inside him. That is true of every individual.

Nestor Makhnor[1]

A silver lining is found in the insufferable *authoritarian philanthropy* that plagued the world between 2020-2022. The unprecedented infringements by the hands of government upon people's liberty has kindled a new-aged renaissance. An awakening, or enlightenment, which is rediscovering the true essence of freedom; a liberty separated from government and collectivist, authoritarian conceptions of society. A liberty that is not constrained nor distorted by the morality of authoritarians and "democratically" appointed men who bestow upon themselves the title of *leader*.

During the covid vaccination crusade, the threads of liberty were sewn with ease – for a child needed only to turn on the television to see the emperor standing proudly without clothing. There truly never has been a better time in history to observe government officials threatening daily lockdowns upon millions, in the name of safety and security, while announcing that *they*, the "leaders of mankind," were generously returning and bestowing upon the people their freedoms. To quote New Zealand's Prime Minister Jacinda

Ardern, who infamously reassured her subjects that they "can now see family and friends again in their homes and use the bathroom inside."[2] The prime minister's comments were televised nationally on November 29, 2021, following the announcement of New Zealand's "My Vaccine Pass."[3] In a bout of poetic irony, Jacinda Arden tested positive for covid-19 on May 13, 2022 – two years into her tyrannical campaign. I shall let that speak for itself.

The blatant lording by these *elected rulers* proved to only weaken the government's self-proclaimed legitimacy to the populace it pretends to represent. The covid vaccine mandates and passports, alongside lockdowns, led many to rescind their faith both in their democratic system and the constitution they once believed would protect them. The war waged on covid effectively broke the spell that democracy had placed; no longer was "democratic" synonymous with "free."

Vaccine passports were immoral, unscientific, and legally abhorrent. That much this book has demonstrated. They dehumanized every aspect of our humanity, fragmented our existence, and forcefully granted the State fundamental components of our autonomy that we once considered inalienable. Segregation of any kind, based on any status may it be racial, class, or medical is unacceptable. It is also important to remember that segregation is dangerous not only for the oppressed but the oppressor; not only for the segregated, but he who segregates. No good has befell a society built upon the misfortunes of others.

If the spectacle of vaccine passports is to continue for the foreseeable future, I implore my fellow readers to be on the right side of history, to tolerate your neighbours regardless of their individual or societally ordained status, and to never succumb to the toxins of cowardice and fear. I will end with the words and spirit of the late Ludwig Von Mises, a prominent classical liberalist scholar, economist, and historian. Ludwig wisely cautioned that any who wish to exchange liberty for prosperity will inevitably find themselves left with neither. He referred to this exchange, and any sort that dares barter with liberty, as a "poor bargain."[4] If there is one takeaway from the entirety of this book, it is that vaccine passports, and anything of the like, will always be deemed a poor bargain.

Chapter 10

FINAL THOUGHTS

> *My political opinions lean more and more to Anarchy (philosoph-*
> *ically understood, meaning the abolition of control not whiskered*
> *men with bombs) ...the most improper job of any man, even*
> *saints...is bossing other men. Not one in a million is fit for it, and*
> *least of all those who seek the opportunity.*
>
> *J.R.R. Tolkien*[1]

This book first began as a short essay written during the summer of 2020, months into one of many Canadian lockdowns. At first, it was a therapeutic endeavour; I felt myself going mad at a time when it seemed no one was speaking up. It was as though the matrix had enveloped humanity whole. The bonds of those whom I spent two decades of my life with shattered as their doors shuttered – simply because the government had ordered them so. All around the world bonds were broken by the silence that followed the segregation of those who dared say *no*.

What started off as a short essay, however, began to grow as I decided to document much of what was happening and what was being said. It was at the time so surreal that I believed it a comedy, and I was determined to not let the government distort once again the telling of history. The notion of a vaccine passport was too great an atrocity to let it be rationalized and assimilated into the human psyche. A life governed by vaccine passports – where your liberty is conditional on your repeated obedience to medical injections – is not one worth living.

I continued to document, more specifically, the introduction of vaccine passports and its consequences from its birth to its seemingly temporary demise. The arguments that were peddled by those who advocated for vaccine passports were also so dystopian that I was compelled to rebuke them privately on a page that I never initially expected anyone to read. As I said, much of it was therapeutic – and speaking of therapy, I reckon an actual therapist would have simply told me to do my part and vaccinate so that my troubles would vanish. That would be the case if I would have even been allowed to walk into a therapy session *unvaccinated*.

The days turned to months and over two years had passed. The dozen page essay I had once written expanded into the book you are reading today. At the time of writing this concluding section, vaccine passports have largely dwindled and faded throughout the world following unprecedented movements of resistance. In the regions that vaccine passports remain, they are no longer so blatantly praised as they once were and resistance towards them only continues to grow. I could have published this book sooner to ease the minds of those who may have, for a time, felt as alone as I did in the absurdity of what transpired. However, I believed it best to wait and create something that could fully capture one of the most inhumane government interventions in human history. In the hopelessness of perpetual fear mongering and heavy-handed government decree, I entrusted humanity to find their senses. I was not disappointed. The protests against vaccine passports and government decrees that gatekept liberties behind the acceptance of pharmaceutical injections, witnessed in Canada and around the world, was a phenomenon never seen before. The voices that were imprisoned for two years re-united and roared with thunderous might. I was there the first week-end in Ottawa for the convoy, initially not knowing what to expect, and it will remain an experience that I will never forget. Neither will the lies of the media on that weekend be forgotten.

The screams of freedom heard from around the world kindled a movement that I believed, for a moment, withered in the matrix of conformity and obedience. I am not only speaking of the movement for liberty but the movement for human connection itself. Like the late J.R.R. Tolkien, who grew to detest the State, I cannot any longer view the world the same following these last two years – nor can I remain blind to a system governed by violence and corrupted by power and control. It is my wish that the liberty movement sparked by the *war on covid* remain determined, lest history repeat itself, to abolish these systems of control rather than to hopelessly "reform" them. For the preservation of liberty and the spirit of human connec-tion, history ought to admonish the notion of vaccine passports and hold accountable the institutions that enabled its creation.

Notes

CHAPTER 1. WHAT HAPPENED?

1.   C. S. Lewis, "The Humanitarian Theory of Punishment," *Issues in Religion and Psychotherapy* 13, no. 1 (1987): 151, Association of Mormon Counselors and Psychotherapists.

CHAPTER 2. INTRODUCTION

1.   "Handout I: Edward R. Murrow, See It Now, March 9, 1954," Bill of Rights Institute, accessed May 30, 2022, https://billofrightsinstitute.org/activities/handout-i-edward-r-murrow-see-it-now-march-9-1954.

CHAPTER 3. GOVERNMENT-INDUCED COMPLIANCE

1.   Thomas S. Szasz, *The Untamed Tongue: A Dissenting Dictionary* (La Salle, Illinois: Open Court, 1991).

2.   "Frequently Asked Questions," Occupational Safety and Health Administration, accessed May 30, 2022, https://www.osha.gov/coronavirus/faqs.

3.   The White House, "Remarks by President Biden at Virtual Meeting on Military Deployments Supporting Hospitals for the COVID-19 Response," January 13, 2022, https://www.whitehouse.gov/briefing-room/speeches-re-marks/2022/01/13/remarks-by-president-biden-at-virtual-meet-ing-on-military-deployments-supporting-hospitals-for-the-covid-19-response/.

4. Rebecca Coombes and Madlen Davies, "Facebook Versus the BMJ: When Fact Checking Goes Wrong," *BMJ* 376, no. 8322 (January 19, 2022): 5, https://doi.org/10.1136/bmj.o95.

5. Joseph Simonson, "How the CDC Coordinated with Big Tech to Censor," *The Washington Free Beacon*, July 27, 2022, https://freebeacon.com/biden-administration/how-the-cdc-co-ordinated-with-big-tech-to-censor-americans/.

6. Michiel Willems, "Blackrock and Vanguard Rake in Billions: Omicron Variant Makes Moderna and Pfizer Shareholders More than $10bn," *City A.M.*, December 6, 2021, https://www.cityam.com/blackrock-and-vanguard-rake-in-billions-omicron-variant-made-moderna-and-pfizer-shareholders-10bn-in-a-week/.

7. Wolfgang Schivelbusch, *Three New Deals Reflections on Roosevelt's America, Mussolini's Italy, and Hitler's Germany, 1933-1939* (New York: Metropolitan Books, 2006), 29.

8. Ibid., 32

9. Ibid., 31

10. Ibid., 23

11. Ibid., 24

12. Ibid., 35

13. Rachel Gilmore, "As Unvaccinated Workers Sue for Wrongful Dismissal, Ottawa Working on Shielding Employers," *Global News*, January 20, 2022,

https://globalnews.ca/news/8523534/covid-omicron-vaccine-mandate-lawsuit-employer-trudeau/.

14. Lisa Kennedy Montgomery, "Episode 151," Kennedy, Fox Business Network, Manhattan, NY: FBN, August 3, 2021.

15. Alyshah Hasham, "Ontario Juries Must Be Vaccinated Starting Next Week," *Toronto Star*, September 1, 2021, https://www.thestar.com/news/gta/2021/09/01/ontario-juries-must-be-vaccinated-starting-next-week.html.

16. Joe Lofaro, "'It Sets a Certain Precedent': Quebec Judge Suspends Unvaccinated Father's Visitation Rights with Child," *CTV News Montreal*, January 12, 2022, https://montreal.ctvnews.ca/it-sets-a-certain-precedent-quebec-judge-suspends-unvaccinated-father-s-visitation-rights-with-child-1.5737271.

17. Ibid.

18. Gary Dimmock, "Judge Bans Ottawa Mother from Advising Son against COVID-19 Vaccine," *Ottawa Citizen*, October 24, 2021, https://ottawacitizen.com/news/local-news/judge-bans-ottawa-mother-from-advising-son-against-covid-19-vaccine.

19. Jacques Poitras, "Unvaccinated New Brunswick Dad Loses Custody of at-Risk Child," *CBC News*, February 4, 2022, https://www.cbc.ca/news/canada/new-brunswick/unvaccinated-dad-loses-custody-of-at-risk-child-1.6338484.

20. Ben Doherty, "Novak Djokovic Visa: Australian Minister Alex Hawke Says Risk of 'Civil Unrest' behind Cancellation," *The Guardian*, January 15, 2022, https://www.theguardian.com/sport/2022/jan/15/novak-djokovic-visa-australian-

minister-alex-hawke-says-risk-of-civil-unrest-behind-cancella-tion.

21. Ibid.

22. "US Science Teacher Arrested for Vaccinating 17-Year-Old Stu-dent," *BBC News*, January 5, 2022, https://www.bbc.com/news/world-us-canada-59876583.

23. Teaganne Finn, "Sens. Elizabeth Warren and Cory Booker Test Positive for Covid," *NBC News*, December 19, 2021, https://www.nbcnews.com/politics/congress/sen-elizabeth-warren-tests-positive-covid-breakthrough-case-n1286289.

24. Ibid.

25. Victoria Albert and Jordan Freiman, "Barack Obama Says He Tested Positive for COVID-19," *CBS News*, March 13, 2022, https://www.cbsnews.com/news/barack-obama-tests-positive-covid-19/.

26. Jonathan Franklin, "Bill Gates Tests Positive for COVID-19, Says He's Experiencing Mild Symptoms," *NPR*, May 10, 2022, https://www.npr.org/2022/05/10/1098066371/bill-gates-positive-covid.

27. "Trudeau Isolating after Testing Positive for COVID-19 Again," *CBC News*, June 13, 2022, https://www.cbc.ca/news/politics/tru-deau-covid-tests-positive-1.6486802.

28. Joanne Lavoie, "Toronto's Medical Officer of Health Contracts COVID-19," *CP24*, June 15, 2022, https://www.cp24.com/news/toronto-s-medical-officer-of-health-contracts-covid-19-1.5947774.

29. Mariana Mazzucato, "Op-Ed: How Taxpayers Prop up Big Pharma, and How to Cap That," *Los Angeles Times*, October 27, 2015, https://www.latimes.com/opinion/op-ed/la-oe-1027-mazzucato-big-pharma-prices-20151027-story.html.

30. Yair Holtzman, "U.S. Research and Development Tax Credit," *The CPA Journal*, October 25, 2017, https://www.cpajournal.com/2017/10/30/u-s-research-development-tax-credit/.

31. Lisa M. Schwartz and Steven Woloshin, "Medical Marketing in the United States, 1997-2016." *JAMA* 321, no. 1 (2019): 80–96, https://doi.org/10.1001/jama.2018.19320.

32. Robin Feldman, "May Your Drug Price Be Evergreen." *Journal of Law and the Biosciences* 5, no. 3 (2018): 590–647, https://doi.org/10.1093/jlb/lsy022.

33. Denis G. Arnold, Oscar Jerome Stewart, and Tammy Beck, "Financial Penalties Imposed on Large Pharmaceutical Firms for Illegal Activities," *JAMA* 324, no. 19 (2020): 1995, https://doi.org/10.1001/jama.2020.18740.

34. Ibid.

35. Ibid.

36. Ibid., 1996.

37. Olivier J. Wouters, "Lobbying Expenditures and Campaign Contributions by the Pharmaceutical and Health Product Industry in the United States, 1999-2018," *JAMA Internal Medicine* 180, no. 5 (2020): 688–97, https://doi.org/10.1001/jamainternmed.2020.0146.

38. Pfizer Inc., 2021 Annual Report, accessed April 1, 2022, https://s28.q4cdn.com/781576035/files/doc_financials/2021/ar/PFE-2021-Form-10K-FINAL.pdf, 51.

39. Ibid., 103.

40. "Pfizer Reports First-Quarter 2022 Results," Business Wire, May 3, 2022, https://www.businesswire.com/news/home/20220502005731/en/.

41. Judy Stone, "The People's Vaccine — Moderna's Coronavirus Vaccine Was Largely Funded by Taxpayer Dollars," *Forbes*, December 3, 2020, https://www.forbes.com/sites/judystone/2020/12/03/the-peoples-vaccine-modernas-coronavirus-vaccine-was-largely-funded-by-taxpayer-dollars/?sh=27283fc96303.

42. Ladna Mohamed, "Gananoque, Ont. Town Councillor Suspended for Criticizing Proof of Vaccination Requirements - Kingston," *Global News*, December 23, 2021, https://globalnews.ca/news/8471528/gananoque-town-councillor-suspended/.

43. Ryan Smith, "'Black Panther' Fans Demand Injured Letitia Wright Is Replaced If She's Unvaccinated," *Newsweek*, November 11, 2021, https://www.newsweek.com/black-panther-fans-demand-injured-letitia-wright-replaced-if-shes-unvaccinated-covid-shuri-cdc-1648328.

44. Zack Linly, "Letitia Wright Leaving Marvel over Vaccine Mandate after Black Panther 2," *NewsOne*, December 10, 2021, https://newsone.com/4258685/letitia-wight-marvel-vaccine-mandate-report/.

45. "Bolsonaro: Brazilian Supreme Court Opens Investigation into Vaccine Comments," *BBC*, December 4, 2021, https://www.bbc.com/news/world-latin-america-59528857.

CHAPTER 4. BUILDING BLOCKS TO VACCINE UNIFORMITY

1. Bertrand Russell, *The Impact of Science on Society* (New York, N.Y.: AMS Press,1993), 29-30

2. "More Polio Cases Now Caused by Vaccine Than by Wild Virus," *Associated Press*, November 25, 2019, https://apnews.com/article/health-united-nations-ap-top-news-pakistan-international-news-7d8b0e32efd0480fbd12acf27729f6a5.

3. Andrew F. Read et al., "Imperfect Vaccination Can Enhance the Transmission of Highly Virulent Pathogens," *PLOS Biology* 13, no. 7 (2015): 1, https://doi.org/10.1371/journal.pbio.1002198.

4. Ibid.

5. Roberta Alexander, "'Leaky' Vaccines Can Produce Stronger Versions of Viruses," *Healthline Media*, April 5, 2019, https://www.healthline.com/health-news/leaky-vaccines-can-produce-stronger-versions-of-viruses-072715.

6. Ibid.

7. Barbara K. Kennedy, "Some Vaccines Support Evolution of More-Virulent Viruses," Penn State University, last modified July 29, 2015, https://www.psu.edu/news/research/story/some-vaccines-support-evolution-more-virulent-viruses/.

Notes

8. Ibid.

9. Ibid.

10. Public Health and Medical Professionals for Transparency v. Food and Drug Administration, 4:21-CV-01058 (N.D. Tex. 2021).

11. Jason Waterman, "Diphtheria in the United States," *Public Health Reports (1896-1970)* 42, no. 40 (1927): 2443, https://doi.org/10.2307/4578516.

12. Ibid.

13. Ibid.

14. C. C. Dauer, "Reported Whooping Cough Morbidity and Mortality in the United States," *Public Health Reports (1896-1970)* 58, no. 17 (1943): 661, https://doi.org/10.2307/4584441.

15. Jamie Bartram and Sandy Cairncross, "Hygiene, Sanitation, and Water: Forgotten Foundations of Health," *PLoS Medicine* 7, no. 11 (2010): e10003671, https://doi.org/10.1371/journal.pmed.1000367.

16. Ibid.

17. Ibid.

18. Ibid.

19. Hillard Kaplan et al., "Coronary Atherosclerosis in Indigenous South American Tsimané: A Cross-Sectional Cohort Study," *The Lancet* 389, no. 10080 (2017): 1730–39,

https://doi.org/10.1016/s0140-6736(17)30752-3.

20. Brea McCauley, "Life Expectancy in Hunter-Gatherers," in *Encyclopedia of Evolutionary Psychological Science*, ed., T. K. Shackelford and V. A. Weekes-Shackelford (Cham, Switzerland: Springer Publishing, 2018), 1-3.

21. Frédéric Bastiat, *The Law*, trans. Dean Russell (Irvington, New York City: Foundation for Economic Education, 1998), 22.

22. Murray N. Rothbard, *The Progressive Era*, ed. Patrick Newman (Auburn, Alabama: Mises Institute, 2017), 297.

23. Bridget Balch, "The Vaccines and the Variants: Four Keys to Ending the Pandemic, "Association of American Medical Colleges, last modified June 9, 2021, https://www.aamc.org/news-insights/vaccines-and-variants-four-keys-ending-pandemic.

CHAPTER 5. VACCINE PASSPORTS: MORALLY INDEFENSIBLE

1. George Orwell, *1984* (London, England: Penguin Books, 2008), 226.

2. John William Perrin, "The History of Compulsory Education in New England" (PhD diss., University of Chicago, 1896), 7-8.

3. Michael Kowalik, "Ethics of Vaccine Refusal," *Journal of Medical Ethics* 48, no. 4 (2022): 240, https://doi.org/10.1136/medethics-2020-107026.

4. "Human Dignity," The Center for Bioethics & Human Dignity, Trinity International University, accessed July 16, 2022, https://cbhd.org/category/issues/human-dignity.

5. "About," Global Dignity Canada, accessed October 28, 2020, https://globaldignity.ca/about/.

6. Murray N. Rothbard, For a New Liberty: The Libertarian Manifesto (Auburn, Alabama: Mises Institute, 2020), 3.

7. Ibid., 60.

8. Ibid., 52.

9. Ibid., 34

10. Ibid., 41.

11. Ibid., 45

12. Thomas Escritt, "Unvaccinated Should Reflect on Their Duty to Society, Merkel Says," *Reuters*, November 12, 2021, https://www.reuters.com/world/europe/unvaccinated-should-reflect-their-duty-society-merkel-says-2021-11-11/.

13. Lloyd Steffen, "The Unvaccinated Owe a Figurative Debt to Society That Should Be Literal," *The Hill*, January 25, 2022, https://thehill.com/opinion/healthcare/591257-the-unvaccinated-owe-a-figurative-debt-to-society-that-should-be-literal.

14. Alek Korab, "Dr. Fauci Just Said This about Your 'Individual Freedom,'" *Yahoo Life*, October 7, 2021, https://ca.style.yahoo.com/dr-fauci-just-said-individual-121519548.html.

15. Rothbard, *For a New Liberty*, 67.

16. Ibid.

17. Henry Hazlitt, *Man vs. The Welfare State* (New Rochelle, New York: Arlington House, 1970), 190.

18. Rothbard, *For a New Liberty*, 73.

19. Ibid., 67.

20. Ibid., 72.

21. Julie Ponesse, *My Choice: The Ethical Case Against COVID-19 Vaccine Mandates* (Toronto, Ontario: The Democracy Fund, 2021), 50.

22. Centers For Disease Control and Prevention, "CDC Expands Eligibility for COVID-19 Booster Shots to All Adults," CDC press release, November 19, 2021, https://www.cdc.gov/media/releases/2021/s1119-booster-shots.html.

23. Centers For Disease Control and Prevention, "CDC Strengthens Recommendations and Expands Eligibility for COVID-19 Booster Shots," CDC press release, May 19, 2022, https://www.cdc.gov/media/releases/2022/s0519-covid-booster-acip.html.

24. Centers For Disease Control and Prevention, "CDC Endorses ACIP's Updated COVID-19 Vaccine Recommendations," CDC press release, December 16, 2021, https://www.cdc.gov/media/releases/2021/s1216-covid-19-vaccines.html.

25. Centers For Disease Control and Prevention, "CDC Recommends COVID-19 Vaccines for Young Children," CDC press release, June 18th, 2022, https://www.cdc.gov/media/releases/2022/s0618-children-vaccine.html.

26. "About," Franny Strong Foundation, 2020, https://frannys-trong.org/our-story/.

27. Ibid.

28. Thomas Gerbet, "Dans L'ombre, La Firme McKinsey était Au Cœur De La Gestion De La Pandémie Au Québec," *Radio Canada*, September 30, 2022, https://ici.radio-can-ada.ca/nouvelle/1920666/mckinsey-quebec-covid-legault-ges-tion-pandemie.

29. Ibid.

30. Ibid.

31. Ibid.

32. "Corporations Benefited Most from Covid Wage Subsidies," *Western Standard*, May 3, 2022, https://www.westernstand-ard.news/news/corporations-benefited-most-from-covid-wage-subsidies/article_a028c3f2-a1ae-5d0f-bc9b-2871f52dcd17.html.

33. Ibid.

34. "Opposition to Mandatory Vaccinations Is 'Irresponsible' and 'Dangerous,' Says Trudeau," *Radio Canada International*, August 20, 2021, https://ici.radio-canada.ca/rci/en/news/1818142/con-servative-opposition-to-mandatory-vaccinations-is-irresponsi-ble-and-dangerous-says-trudeau.

35. Sean O'Grady, "This Is What We Do about Anti-Vaxxers: No Job. No Entry. No NHS Access," *The Independent*, May 18, 2021, https://www.independent.co.uk/voices/antivaxxers-vaccine-

coronavirus-nhs-b1849437.html.

36. Molly Nagle, "Fauci Warns 'Things Are Going to Get Worse' with COVID," *ABC News*, August 1, 2021, https://abcnews.go.com/Politics/fauci-warns-things-worse-covid/story?id=79192069.

37. The White House, "Press Briefing by Press Secretary Jen Psaki," December 1, 2021, https://www.whitehouse.gov/brief-ing-room/press-briefings/2021/12/01/press-briefing-by-press-secretary-jen-psaki-december-1-2021/.

38. Melissa Frick, "'You People Are Just Vectors of Disease to Me': Ferris State Professor Goes on Curse-Filled Rant during Lecture," *Mlive*, January 28, 2022, https://www.mlive.com/news/grand-rapids/2022/01/you-peo-ple-are-just-vectors-of-disease-to-me-ferris-state-professor-goes-on-curse-filled-rant-during-lecture.html.

39. G.K. Bowes, "Epidemic Disease: Past, Present and Future," *Journal of the Royal Sanitary Institute* 66, no. 3 (1946): 174-179, https://doi.org/10.1177/146642404606600302.

40. Arthur Allen, *Vaccine: The Controversial Story of Medicines Greatest Lifesaver* (New York City, New York: W. W. Norton, 2007), 69.

41. Kristoffer Mousten Hansen, "Smallpox: The Historical Myths behind Mandatory Vaccines," Mises Wire, Mises Institute, last modified November 24, 2021, https://mises.org/wire/smallpox-historical-myths-behind-mandatory-vaccines.

42. Renee Anushka Alli, ed., "Side Effects of the Smallpox Vaccine," *WebMD*, December 20, 2020,

https://www.webmd.com/a-to-z-guides/smallpox-vaccination-effects.

43. Suzanne Humphries and Roman Bystrianyk, *Dissolving Illusions: Disease, Vaccines, and The Forgotten History* (Scotts Valley, California: CreateSpace Independent Publishing Platform, 2013).

44. Ibid.

45. *Zucht v. King*, 260 U.S. 174 (1922).

46. *Plessy v. Ferguson*, 163 U.S. 537 (1896).

47. Public Health Agency of Canada, *Canadian National Report on Immunization, 1996*, May 1997, 3, https://publications.gc.ca/collections/collection_2016/aspc-phac/HP3-1-23-S4-eng.pdf.

48. Ibid.

49. Ibid.

50. Marlene L. Durand et al., "Acute Bacterial Meningitis in Adults – a Review of 493 Episodes," *New England Journal of Medicine* 328, no. 1 (1993): 21–28, https://doi.org/10.1056/nejm199301073280104.

51. Lisa Lockerd Maragakis, "COVID-19 vs. The Flu," Johns Hopkins Medicine, John Hopkins University, February 23, 2022, https://www.hopkinsmedicine.org/health/conditions-and-diseases/coronavirus/coronavirus-disease-2019-vs-the-flu.

52. John Paget et al., "Global Mortality Associated with Seasonal Influenza Epidemics: New Burden Estimates and Predictors

from the Glamor Project." *Journal of Global Health* 9, no. 2 (2019): 020421, https://doi.org/10.7189/jogh.09.020421.

53. Amanda MacMillan, "Hospitals Overwhelmed by Flu Patients Are Treating Them in Tents," *TIME*, January 18, 2018, https://time.com/5107984/hospitals-handling-burden-flu-patients/.

54. Canadian Institute for Health Information, *Care in Canadian ICUs*, August 2016, 26, https://secure.cihi.ca/free_products/ICU_Report_EN.pdf.

55. Ibid., 27.

56. Ian Hamilton, "Hospital Beds Needed for Coronavirus Victims Are Being Blocked by Alcoholics Depending on the NHS," *The Independent*, April 13, 2020, https://www.independent.co.uk/voices/coronavirus-hospital-beds-crisis-nhs-alcohol-death-treatment-failure-a9462156.html.

57. Rachel Gilmore, "Trudeau Unveils Canada's International Proof-of-Vaccination for COVID-19," *Global News*, October 21, 2021, https://globalnews.ca/news/8286078/covid-coronavirus-vaccine-passport-certificate-federal-travel/.

58. Office of the Premier," Ontario Moving to Next Phase of Reopening on February 17," news release, February 14, 2022, https://news.ontario.ca/en/release/1001600/ontario-moving-to-next-phase-of-reopening-on-february-17.

59. Centers for Disease Control and Prevention, *Interim Operational Considerations for Implementing the Shielding Approach to Prevent COVID-19 Infections in Humanitarian Settings*, July 29, 2020, 4-6, https://www.cdc.gov/coronavirus/2019-

ncov/downloads/global-covid-19/Interim-Operational-Consid-
erations-Implementing-Shielding-in-Humanitarian-Set-
tings.pdf.

60. Ibid., 5.

CHAPTER 6. VACCINE PASSPORTS: THE SCIENCE

1. Chris Clemens, "Christianity in Scientific Mythology," Society
   of Catholic Scientists, September 10, 2019, https://catholicscien-
   tists.org/articles/christian-truth-in-an-age-of-scientific-mythol-
   ogy/.

2. "Transcript: The Rachel Maddow Show, 3/29/21," *MSNBC*,
   March 29, 2021, https://www.msnbc.com/transcripts/transcript-
   rachel-maddow-show-3-29-21-n1262442.

3. Yasmeen Abutaleb, Carolyn Y. Johnson, and Joel Achenbach,
   "'The War Has Changed': Internal CDC Document Urges New
   Messaging, Warns Delta Infections Likely More Severe," *Washington Post*, August 6, 2021, https://www.washing-
   tonpost.com/health/2021/07/29/cdc-mask-guidance/.

4. Madeline Holcombe, "Fully Vaccinated People Who Get a
   Covid-19 Breakthrough Infection Can Transmit the Virus, CDC
   Chief Says," *CNN*, August 6, 2021,
   https://www.cnn.com/2021/08/05/health/us-coronavirus-thurs-
   day/index.html.

5. Anika Singanayagam et al., "Community Transmission and Viral Load Kinetics of the SARS-CoV-2 Delta (B.1.617.2) Variant
   in Vaccinated and Unvaccinated Individuals in the UK: A Pro-
   spective, Longitudinal, Cohort Study," *The Lancet Infectious*

Diseases 22, no. 2 (October 29, 2021): 183–95. https://doi.org/10.1016/s1473-3099(21)00648-4.

6. Robert Hart, "Pfizer's Covid Vaccine Protection against Omicron Fades Just Weeks after Second and Third Doses, Study Finds," *Forbes*, May 13, 2022, https://www.forbes.com/sites/roberthart/2022/05/13/pfizers-covid-vaccine-protection-against-omicron-fades-just-weeks-after-second-and-third-doses-study-finds/?sh=214e4c0932af.

7. Aria Bendix, "BA.5, Now Dominant U.S. Variant, May Pose the Biggest Threat to Immune Protection Yet," *NBC News*, July 7, 2022, https://www.nbcnews.com/health/health-news/omicron-ba5-ba4-covid-symptoms-vaccines-rcna36894.

8. Elizabeth Stuart and Sarah Boxer, "Cornell University Reports More Than 900 Covid-19 Cases This Week. Many Are Omicron Variant Cases in Fully Vaccinated Students," *CNN*, December 16, 2021, https://amp.cnn.com/cnn/2021/12/14/us/cornell-university-covid-cases/index.html.

9. Andy Rose and Francesca Street, "48 Test Positive for Covid on World's Biggest Cruise Ship," *CNN*, December 21, 2021, https://www.cnn.com/travel/article/cruise-ship-royal-caribbean-covid/index.html.

10. Ibid.

11. James Dator, "The NFL's Covid Outbreak Is Absolutely out of Control," SB Nation, Vox Media, last modified December 17, 2021, https://www.sbnation.com/nfl/2021/12/17/22840941/nfl-covid-outbreak-browns-raiders.

12. "Frequently Asked Questions about COVID-19 Vaccination,"

CDC, July 20, 2022, https://www.cdc.gov/coronavirus/2019-ncov/vaccines/faq.html.

13. Trevor Hunnicutt, "First Known U.S. Omicron Case Found in Fully Vaccinated Overseas Traveler," *Reuters*, December 1, 2021, https://www.reuters.com/business/healthcare-pharmaceuticals/us-reports-first-case-omicron-variant-2021-12-01/.

14. "COVID-19 Vaccines Work," CDC, June 28, 2022, https://www.cdc.gov/coronavirus/2019-ncov/vaccines/effectiveness/work.html.

15. Jon Wertheim, "Mailbag: Are Tennis Players Getting Vaccinated," *Sports Illustrated*, July 21, 2021, https://www.si.com/tennis/2021/07/21/tennis-players-vaccinations-olympics-djokavic-federer-barty.

16. Maggie Fox, "Unvaccinated People Are 'Variant Factories,' Infectious Diseases Expert Says," *CNN*, July 3, 2021, https://www.cnn.com/2021/07/03/health/unvaccinated-variant-factories/index.html.

17. Paul Elias Alexander, "150 Plus Research Studies Affirm Naturally Acquired Immunity to Covid-19: Documented, Linked, and Quoted," Brownstone Institute, October 17, 2021, https://brownstone.org/articles/79-research-studies-affirm-naturally-acquired-immunity-to-covid-19-documented-linked-and-quoted/.

18. Christian Holm Hansen et al., "Assessment of Protection against Reinfection with SARS-CoV-2 among 4 Million PCR-Tested Individuals in Denmark in 2020: A Population-Level Observational," *The Lancet* 397, no. 10280 (March 17, 2021): 1204-1212, https://doi.org/10.1016/s0140-6736(21)00575-4.

19. Jeffrey Klausner and Noah Kojima, "Op-Ed: Quit Ignoring Natural COVID Immunity," *Medpage Today*, May 28, 2021, https://www.medpagetoday.com/infectiousdisease/covid19/92836.

20. Zijun Wang et al., "Naturally Enhanced Neutralizing Breadth against SARS-Cov 2 One Year After," *Nature* 595, no. 7867 (June 14, 2021): 426-431, https://doi.org/10.1038/s41586-021-03696-9.

21. Sivan Gazit et al., "Comparing SARS-CoV-2 Natural Immunity to Vaccine-Induced Immunity: Reinfections Versus Breakthrough Infections," *medRxiv*, August 25, 2021, https://doi.org/10.1101/2021.08.24.21262415.

22. Thomas M. León et al., COVID-19 Cases and Hospitalizations by COVID-19 Vaccination Status and Previous COVID-19 Diagnosis — California and New York, May– November 2021," *Morbidity and Mortality Weekly Report* 71, no. 4 (January 28, 2022): 125-131, http://dx.doi.org/10.15585/mmwr.mm7104e1.

23. Rhia Kundu et al., "Cross-Reactive Memory T Cells Associate with Protection against SARS-COV-2 Infection in COVID-19 Contacts," *Nature Communications* 13, no. 80 (January 10, 2022), https://doi.org/10.1038/s41467-021-27674-x.

24. Daniel Lozano-Ojalvo et al., "Differential Effects of the Second SARS-COV-2 mRNA Vaccine Dose on T Cell Immunity in Naive and COVID-19 Recovered Individuals," *Cell Reports* 36, no. 8 (August 24, 2021): 109570, https://doi.org/10.1016/j.celrep.2021.109570.

25. Kaia Hubbard, "Fauci Says It's a Matter of 'When, Not if' the Definition of Fully Vaccinated Will Change," *U.S. News &*

World Report, December 8, 2021, https://www.us-news.com/news/health-news/articles/2021-12-08/fauci-says-its-a-matter-of-when-not-if-the-definition-of-fully-vaccinated-will-change.

26. Jeannie Baumann, "Up-to-Date Shots Encouraged over 'Fully Vaccinated': Fauci (1)," *Bloomberg Law*, January 4, 2022, https://news.bloomberglaw.com/health-law-and-business/up-to-date-shots-replacing-term-fully-vaccinated-fauci-says.

27. "Dr. Anthony Fauci on the Threat from Omicron: 'if You Want to Be Fully Protected, Get Boosted,'" *CBS News*, December 30, 2021, https://www.cbsnews.com/news/anthony-fauci-covid-vaccine-booster-omicron/.

28. "Prime Minister's Address to the Nation on Booster Jabs: 12 December 2021," Government of the United Kingdom, December 12, 2021, https://www.gov.uk/government/speeches/prime-ministers-address-to-the-nation-on-booster-jabs-12-december-2021.

29. The White House, "Press Briefing by White House COVID-19 Response Team and Public Health Officials," July 12, 2022, https://www.whitehouse.gov/briefing-room/press-briefings/2022/07/12/press-briefing-by-white-house-covid-19-response-team-and-public-health-officials-87/.

30. The Canadian Press, "Trudeau Says Boosting Vaccination Efforts, Coming to Terms with 'Historical Wrongs' among 2022 Priorities," *CBC News*, January 1, 2022, https://www.cbc.ca/news/politics/trudeau-year-end-1.6301791.

31. Katie Dangerfield, "Canada Set to Receive 35M Pfizer COVID-19 Booster Vaccines for 2022," *Global News*, April 23, 2021,

https://globalnews.ca/news/7783486/covid-canada-pfizer-booster-vaccine/.

32. Gerrard Kaonga, "Netherlands Announces Plan to Give People up to Six Doses of COVID Vaccine," *Newsweek*, December 31, 2021, https://www.newsweek.com/netherlands-vaccination-booster-coronavirus-covid-shot-1664296.

33. "Pfizer CEO Says an Annual Covid Vaccine Is Preferable to Periodic Boosters," *Reuters*, January 22, 2022, https://www.cnbc.com/2022/01/22/pfizer-ceo-says-an-annual-covid-vaccine-is-preferable-to-periodic-boosters.html.

34. Paul Sacca, "Bill Gates – Who Caught COVID despite 4 Shots – Says People over Age 50 Need Vaccine Boosters Every 6 Months, Calls Popular Conspiracy Theory about Him 'Tragic'," *Blaze Media*, May 15, 2022, https://www.theblaze.com/news/bill-gates-covid-vaccine-conspiracy-theory?utm_source=dlvr.it&utm_medium=twitter.

35. "Remarks for the Honourable Jean-Yves Duclos Minister of Health," Public Health Agency of Canada, June 30, 2022, https://www.canada.ca/en/public-health/news/2022/07/remarks-for-the-honourable-jean-yves-duclos-minister-of-health.html.

36. Ibid.

37. Akiko Iwasaki and Albert Ko, "Why You'll Need to Get COVID-19 Boosters Again and Again," *TIME*, July 19, 2022, https://time.com/6198402/covid-19-boosters/.

38. Carol Zimmermann, "COVID-19 Booster Shots to Be Required at Some Catholic Colleges Next Year," *Crux*, December 16,

2021, https://cruxnow.com/church-in-the-usa/2021/12/covid-19-booster-shots-to-be-required-at-some-catholic-colleges-next-year.

39. "COVID-19 Vaccinations," University of Toronto, accessed August 8, 2022, https://www.utoronto.ca/utogether/vaccines.

40. Western Communications, "Western Requires COVID-19 Booster and Masking in Instructional Spaces This Fall," *Western News*, https://news.westernu.ca/2022/08/western-requires-covid-19-booster-masking-instructional-spaces-this-fall/.

41. Dawn Lim, "Blackstone Tells U.S. Staff to Get Boosters or Stay Away," *Bloomberg*, January 12, 2022, https://www.bloomberg.com/news/articles/2022-01-13/blackstone-tells-u-s-staff-to-get-boosters-or-get-out-of-office.

42. Adeshola Ore, "Victoria Stands down 420 Public School Teachers over Vaccine Mandates," *The Guardian*, April 27, 2022, https://www.theguardian.com/australia-news/2022/apr/28/victoria-stands-down-420-public-school-teachers-over-vaccine-mandates.

43. Joe Pinsker, "How to Socialize Safely in the Booster Era," *The Atlantic*, December 6, 2021, https://www.theatlantic.com/family/archive/2021/12/covid-booster-fully-vaccinated-omicron/620916/.

44. Ibid.

45. Maragakis, "COVID-19 vs. The Flu."

46. Molly Murphy and Brian Stryker to Interested Parties, memorandum, "Taking the Win over COVID-19," February 24, 2022,

Impact Research, Children's Health Defense, https://chil-drenshealthdefense.org/wp-content/uploads/IMPACT-COVID-positioning-strategy-memo.pdf.

47. Centers for Disease Control and Prevention, *Risk for COVID-19 Infection, Hospitalization, and Death By Age Group*, last modified June 27, 2022, https://www.cdc.gov/coronavirus/2019-ncov/covid-data/investigations-discovery/hospitalization-death-by-age.html.

48. Christina Yek et al., "Risk Factors for Severe COVID-19 Outcomes among Persons Aged ≥18 Years Who Completed a Primary COVID-19 Vaccination Series — 465 Health Care Facilities, United States, December 2020 – October 2021," *MMWR. Morbidity and Mortality Weekly Report* 71, no. 1 (January 7, 2022): 19–25, https://doi.org/10.15585/mmwr.mm7101a4.

49. David Rutz, "CDC Director's ABC News Interview Remarks about COVID-19 Victims with 'Comorbidities' Spark Confusion," *Fox News*, January 11, 2022, https://www.foxnews.com/media/cdc-director-remarks-comorbities.

50. Amna Nawaz and Courtney Norris, "Older Americans Make up a Majority of COVID Deaths. They Are Falling behind on," *PBS NewsHour*, December 13, 2021, https://www.pbs.org/newshour/show/older-americans-make-up-a-majority-of-covid deaths-they-are-falling-behind-on-boosters.

51. Rachel Roubein and McKenzie Beard, "A Growing Percentage of Americans Dying from Covid-19 Are Vaccinated," *Washington Post*, April 29, 2022, https://www.washingtonpost.com/politics/2022/04/29/growing-percentage-americans-dying-covid-19-are-vaccinated/.

52. Jeffrey H. Anderson, "Let's Shed the Masks and Mandates —
   Omicron Stats Show We Can Stop Living in Fear," *New York
   Post*, January 9, 2022, https://nypost.com/2022/01/09/omicron-
   stats-show-we-dont-need-mask-mandates-or-vaccine-require-
   ments/.

53. Star's Editorial Board, "Time to Raise the Price for Those Who
   Still Won't Get Vaxxed," *Toronto Star*, January 9, 2022,
   https://www.thestar.com/opinion/editorials/2022/01/09/time-
   to-raise-the-price-for-those-who-still-wont-get-vaxxed.html.

54. "Covid: UAE Bans Foreign Travel for Citizens without Booster
   Jab," *BBC News*, January 1, 2022,
   https://www.bbc.com/news/world-middle-east-59845833.

CHAPTER 7. VACCINE PASSPORTS: THE LAW

1. Bastiat, *The* Law, 7.

2. "Universal Declaration on Bioethics and Human Rights," The
   United Nations Educational, Scientific and Cultural Organization, October 19, 2005, https://en.unesco.org/about-us/legal-af-
   fairs/universal-declaration-bioethics-and-human-rights.

3. "The Nuremberg Code (1947)," *BMJ* 313, no. 7070 (1996): 1448,
   https://doi.org/10.1136/bmj.313.7070.1448.

4. "Informed Consent," Canadian Medical Protective Association,
   March 2021, https://www.cmpa-acpm.ca/en/education-
   events/good-practices/physician-patient/informed-consent.

5. Ibid.

6. Ibid.

7. "Universal Declaration of Human Rights," United Nations, December 10, 1948, https://www.un.org/en/about-us/universal-declaration-of-human-rights.

8. Geert De Clercq, "France Hopes New Vaccine Pass Will Speed up Vaccination Amid Omicron Spread," *Reuters*, December 18, 2021, https://www.reuters.com/world/europe/up-10-new-french-covid-19-cases-suspected-be-omicron-variant-minister-2021-12-18/.

9. Oliver Gill, "Ban 'Idiot' Anti-Vaxxers from Flying, Says Ryanair Boss," *The Telegraph*, December 17, 2021, https://www.telegraph.co.uk/business/2021/12/17/ban-idiot-anti-vaxxers-flying-says-ryanair-boss/.

10. Editorial Board, "Time to Raise the Price."

11. Bobbi-Jean MacKinnon, "Province Ponders Proof of Vaccination at Liquor, Cannabis Stores," *CBC News*, January 14, 2022, https://www.cbc.ca/news/canada/new-brunswick/new-brunswick-covid-19-unvaccinated-restrictions-proof-liquor-cannabis-higgs-1.6314439.

12. Rachel Treisman, "Chicago and Boston Will Require Proof of Vaccination in Indoor Settings," *NPR*, December 22, 2021, https://www.npr.org/2021/12/22/1066879001/chicago-and-boston-will-require-proof-of-vaccination-in-indoor-settings.

13. "Macron Declares His Covid Strategy Is to 'Piss off' the Unvaccinated," *The Guardian*, January 4, 2022, https://www.theguardian.com/world/2022/jan/04/macron-declares-his-covid-strategy-is-to-piss-off-the-unvaccinated.

14. Ibid.

15. Dave Naylor, "Trudeau Calls the Unvaccinated Racist and Misogynistic Extremists," *Western Standard*, December 29, 2021, https://www.westernstandard.news/news/trudeau-calls-the-unvaccinated-racist-and-misogynistic-extremists/article_a3bacece-2e14-5b8c-bf37-eddd672205f3.html.

16. Mary Schlangenstein, "Delta Air Lines to Impose Monthly Surcharge on Unvaccinated Employees," Bloomberg, August 25, 2021, https://www.bloomberg.com/news/articles/2021-08-25/delta-air-lines-to-impose-surcharge-on-unvaccinated-employees#xj4y7vzkg.

17. Leslie Josephs, "Delta Hands out Bonuses to Managers Whose Pay Was Cut in the Pandemic," *CNBC*, March 1, 2021, https://www.cnbc.com/2021/03/01/delta-hands-out-bonuses-to-managers-whose-pay-was-cut-in-the-pandemic.html.

18. Leslie Josephs, "Delta Ends $200 Monthly Health Insurance Surcharge on Unvaccinated Employees after Covid Cases Drop," *CNBC*, April 13, 2022, https://www.cnbc.com/2022/04/13/delta-ends-200-health-insurance-surcharge-on-unvaccinated-employees.html.

19. Alexander Coolidge, "Kroger Adds Monthly Surcharge for Unvaccinated Workers, Cuts Their COVID-19 Sick Leave," *USA Today*, December 15, 2021, https://www.usatoday.com/story/money/2021/12/15/kroger-surcharge-covid-unvaccinated-workers/8905191002/.

20. Tabitha Mueller, "State Ends Employee COVID Testing, Rolls Back Fees for Unvaccinated," *The Nevada Independent*, March 24,

2022, https://thenevadaindependent.com/article/state-ends-employee-covid-testing-almost-no-workers-fired-over-vaccine-mandate.

21. Zia Weise, "Austria's Vaccine Mandate to Apply from February 1," *POLITICO*, January 16, 2022, https://www.politico.eu/article/austrias-vaccination-mandate-to-apply-from-february-1/.

22. Ibid.

23. Emily Schultheis and Geir Moulson, "Austrian Parliament Approves Vaccine Mandate for Adults," *ABC News*, January 20, 2022, https://abcnews.go.com/Health/wireStory/austrian-parliament-vote-universal-vaccine-mandate-82368990.

24. Christopher F. Schuetze, "Austria Quietly Discards a Vaccine Mandate That It Never Enforced," June 23, 2022, https://www.nytimes.com/2022/06/23/world/europe/austria-covid-vaccine-mandate.html.

25. Eleni Chrepa, "Greece to Stop Monthly Fines for Unvaccinated Seniors," *Bloomberg*, March 23, 2022, https://www.bloomberg.com/news/articles/2022-03-23/greece-to-stop-monthly-fines-for-unvaccinated-seniors#xj4y7vzkg.

26. "Covid: Italy to Suspend Unvaccinated over-50 Workers," *Wanted in Rome*, February 15, 2022, https://www.wantedinrome.com/news/covid-italy-unvaccinated-workers-over-50.html.

27. Chiara Albanese and Flavia Rotondi, "Italy to End Emergency State Two Years after Pandemic Started," *Bloomberg*, February 23, 2022, https://www.bloomberg.com/news/articles/2022-02-23/italy-to-end-emergency-state-two-years-after-pandemic-

started.

28. "Unvaccinated Workers Who Lose Jobs Ineligible for EI Benefits, Minister Says," *The National Post*, December 13, 2021, https://nationalpost.com/news/canada/unvaccinated-workers-who-lose-jobs-ineligible-for-ei-benefits-barring-exemption-minister-says.

29. Bobby Caina Calvan, "NYC Vaccination Mandate for the Private Sector Takes Effect," *The Associated Press*, December 27, 2021, https://www.usnews.com/news/best-states/new-york/articles/2021-12-27/nyc-vaccination-mandate-for-the-private-sector-takes-effect.

30. Evandro Gigante et a., "New York City Issues Guidance on Private Employer COVID-19 Vaccine Mandate," Law and the Workplace, Proskauer, December 15, 2021. https://www.lawandtheworkplace.com/2021/12/new-york-city-issues-guidance-on-private-employer-covid-19-vaccine-mandate/.

31. Matthew Chayes, "NYC Acknowledges It's Stopped Enforcing Vaccine Mandate for Private Employers," *Newsday*, June 22, 2022, https://www.newsday.com/news/health/coronavirus/new-york-city-mayor-eric-adams-covid-19-vaccine-mandates-tw9kpnmv.

32. Lynn Chaya, "COVID-19 Vaccine Now Mandatory to Get Euthanized in Germany," *National Post*, December 2, 2021, https://nationalpost.com/news/covid-19-vaccine-now-mandatory-to-get-euthanized-in-germany.

33. Ibid.

34. "Covid: I'm Unvaccinated and Can't Get Fertility Treatment," *BBC*, January 8, 2022, https://www.bbc.com/news/uk-scotland-59914425.

35. INS Code-Health Care Expenses, IL HB 4259, 102nd GA. (2022)

36. Rachel Treisman, "Singapore Will Stop Covering the Medical Bills of Unvaccinated COVID-19 Patients," *NPR*, November 9, 2021, https://www.npr.org/sections/coronavirus-live-updates/2021/11/09/1053889069/singapore-medical-bills-covid-19-patients-unvaccinated-by-choice.

37. Verity Stevenson and Isaac Olson, "Unvaccinated Quebecers Will Have to Pay a Health Tax, Legault Says," *CBC News*, January 11, 2022, https://www.cbc.ca/news/canada/montreal/unvaccinated-health-contribution-quebec-1.6311054.

38. Relating to Health and Safety-Immunization Against Covid-19, R.I. SB 2552, GA. (2022).

39. Diane Francis, "Diane Francis: Make the Unvaccinated Pay for Their Own Health Care," *Financial Post*, December 22, 2021, https://financialpost.com/diane-francis/diane-francis-make-the-unvaccinated-pay-for-their-own-health-care.

40. Berkeley Lovelace Jr., "CDC Study Finds about 78% of People Hospitalized for Covid Were Overweight or Obese," *CNBC*, March 9, 2021, https://www.cnbc.com/2021/03/08/covid-cdc-study-finds-roughly-78percent-of-people-hospitalized-were-overweight-or-obese.html.

41. Office of Juvenile Justice and Delinquency Prevention, *Juvenile Arrests 2008*, December 2009, https://www.ojp.gov/pdffiles1/ojjdp/228479.pdf.

42. Andrea Woo, "Unvaccinated Disproportionately Risk Safety of Those Vaccinated against COVID-19, Study Shows," *The Globe and Mail*, April 25, 2022, https://www.theglobe-andmail.com/canada/article-unvaccinated-covid-risk-for-vac-cinated-canada/.

43. Megan Ogilvie, May Warren, and Kenyon Wallace, "Remaining Unvaccinated Increases Risk to the Vaccinated, Says U of T COVID Study," *Toronto Star*, April 25, 2022, https://www.thestar.com/news/gta/2022/04/25/remaining-un-vaccinated-increases-risk-to-the-vaccinated-says-u-of-t-covid-study.html.

44. Canadian Charter of Rights and Freedoms, s 7, Part 1 of the Constitution Act, 1982, being Schedule B to the Canada Act 1982 (UK), 1982, c 11.

45. Ibid.

46. Jeremiah Rodriguez, "Vaccine Hesitancy: StatCan Says Black, Latinx Canadians Least Willing to Take COVID-19 Shot," *CTV News*, April 1, 2021, https://www.ctvnews.ca/health/corona-virus/vaccine-hesitancy-statcan-says-black-latinx-canadians-least-willing-to-take-covid-19-shot-1.5371783.

47. "Black Canadians More Likely to Be Hesitant about COVID-19 Vaccines, Survey Suggests," *CBC*, July 15, 2021, https://www.cbc.ca/news/health/black-canadians-vaccine-hesi-tancy-covid19-1.6102770.

48. Government of Canada, *Government of Canada COVID-19 Update for Indigenous Peoples and Communities, Week of July 19*, accessed July 24, 2021, https://www.canada.ca/en/indigenous-

services-canada/news/2021/07/government-of-canada-covid-19-update-for-indigenous-peoples-and-communities-week-of-july-19.html.

49. "Poverty in Canada," Canadian Poverty Institute, accessed June 4, 2022, https://www.povertyinstitute.ca/poverty-canada.

50. Government of Canada, *Government of Canada COVID-19 Update for Indigenous Peoples and Communities, Week of July 19*, accessed January 25th, 2022, https://www.canada.ca/en/indigenous-services-canada/news/2021/07/government-of-canada-covid-19-update-for-indigenous-peoples-and-communities-week-of-july-19.html.

51. Athena Jones, "Black New Yorkers May Have the Lowest Vaccination Rates, but Community Groups Refuse to Give Up," *CNN*, August 19, 2021, https://www.cnn.com/2021/08/18/us/black-new-yorkers-low-vaccination-rates/index.html.

52. Laura Osman, "Unvaccinated Travellers over the Age of 12 Barred from Planes and Trains as of Today," *CBC News*, November 30, 2021, https://www.cbc.ca/news/politics/unvaccinated-travellers-rules-1.6267648.

53. Canadian Charter of Rights and Freedoms, s 2, Part 1 of the Constitution Act, 1982, being Schedule B to the Canada Act 1982 (UK), 1982, c 11.

54. Joan Bryden and Lina Dib, "MPs Will Need to Be Fully Vaccinated against COVID-19 to Enter House of Commons Next Month," *Global News*, October 20, 2021, https://globalnews.ca/news/8281853/covid-canada-parliament-vaccine-mandate/.

55. Richard Raycraft, "Conservative MP Removed from Parliament Hill over Vaccination Status," *CBC News*, June 3, 2022, https://www.cbc.ca/news/politics/conservative-mp-house-re-moved-1.6477120.

56. *Mouvement laïque québécois v. Saguenay (City)* 2015 SCC 16, [2015] 2 SCR 3.

57. "Section 2(a) – Freedom of Religion," Charterpedia, Department of Justice, last modified April 14, 2022, https://www.jus-tice.gc.ca/eng/csj-sjc/rfc-dlc/ccrf-ccdl/check/art2a.html.

58. C.S. Lewis, *God in The Dock: Essays on Theology and Ethics*, ed. Walter Hooper (Grand Rapids, Michigan: William B. Eerdmans Publishing Company, 1970), 314.

CHAPTER 8. THE OAKES TEST: A SUMMARY

1. Lysander Spooner, *An Essay on the Trial by Jury* (Boston: John P. Jewett and Company; Ohio, Cleveland: Jewett, Proctor & Worthington, 1852, 14.

2. Canadian Charter of Rights and Freedoms, Part I of the Constitution Act, 1982, being Schedule B to the Canada Act 1982 (UK), 1982, c 11, s 1.

3. "COVID-19 Epidemiology Update," Government of Canada, accessed July 25, 2022, https://health-infobase.canada.ca/covid-19/?stat=num&measure=deaths&map=pt.

4. Ibid.

5. Roubein and Beard, "A Growing Percentage of Americans."

6. "Finland's Minister of Justice: Covid-19 Passports' Use Not Justified under Current Situation," Finland's Minister of Justice: COVID-19 Passports' Use Not Justified Under Current Situation, *SchengenVisa News*, February 1, 2022, https://www.schengenvisainfo.com/news/finlands-minister-of-justice-covid-19-passports-use-not-justified-under-current-situation/.

7. "Austria Scraps COVID Vaccine Mandate," *Deutsche Welle*, June 23, 2022, https://www.dw.com/en/austria-scraps-covid-vaccine-mandate/a-62236080.

8. Daniel J. Rowe, "Quebec Reports over 17,000 New COVID-19 Cases to Start 2022," *CTV News Montreal*, January 2, 2022, https://montreal.ctvnews.ca/quebec-reports-over-17-000-new-covid-19-cases-to-start-2022-1.5725162.

9. Bruce Deachman, "COVID-19: Ontario Reports 656 New Cases, 20 in Ottawa; Vaccine Hunters Wind down Ops," *Ottawa Citizen*, September 1, 2021, https://ottawacitizen.com/news/local-news/covid-19-ontario-reports-656-new-cases-22-in-ottawa.

10. "Ontario Reports 18,445 New COVID-19 Cases on New Year's Day, a Pandemic High," *CBC News*, January 1, 2022, https://www.cbc.ca/news/canada/toronto/ontario-covid-cases-new-year-1.6301887.

11. "Ford Calls for Patience as Ontario's Vaccine Certificate System Kicks in, 463 New COVID-19 Cases Logged," *CBC News*, September 22, 2022, https://www.cbc.ca/news/canada/toronto/covid-19-ontario-september-22-2021-update-1.6185071.

12. Stephen Maher January 6, "Trudeau Says Canadians Are 'Angry' at the Unvaccinated," *Macleans*, January 6, 2022,

https://www.macleans.ca/politics/trudeau-says-canadians-are-angry-at-the-unvaccinated/.

13. Anderson, "Let's Shed the Masks and Mandates."

14. Editorial Board, "Time to Raise the Price."

15. Philip Authier, "Legault Drops Idea of Anti-Vax Tax, Citing Need to Preserve Social Peace," *Montreal Gazette*, February 1, 2022, https://montrealgazette.com/news/local-news/legault-is-poised-to-back-away-from-quebecs-anti-vax-tax-report-says.

16. Tristin Hopper, "How COVID-19 Made Canada Comfortable with Marginalizing 3.7 Million People," *National Post*, January 14, 2022, https://nationalpost.com/news/canada/punishing-the-unvaccinated-has-become-one-of-the-most-popular-positions-in-country.

17. Hannah Brown, "'Vaxxed Nation': Film on Israeli COVID Vaccine Program Debuts Next Week," *The Jerusalem Post*, July 18, 2021, https://www.jpost.com/israel-news/culture/vaxxed-nation-film-on-israeli-covid-vaccine-program-debuts-next-week-673319.

18. "Israel Records Highest Daily Rise in Covid Infections," *Agence France-Presse*, January 5, 2022, https://www.france24.com/en/live-news/20220105-israel-records-highest-daily-rise-in-covid-infections.

19. Pete McKenzie, "As Cases Skyrocket, New Zealand Finally Faces Its Covid Reckoning," *The New York Times*, March 3, 2022, https://www.nytimes.com/2022/03/03/world/australia/new-zealand-covid-omicron.html.

20. Anna Jones, "How Did New Zealand Become Covid-19 Free," *BBC*, July 10, 2020, https://www.bbc.com/news/world-asia-53274085.

21. Marisa Penaloza, "New Zealand Declares Victory over Coronavirus Again, Lifts Auckland Restrictions," *NPR*, October 7, 2020, https://www.npr.org/sections/coronavirus-live-updates/2020/10/07/921171807/new-zealand-declares-victory-over-coronavirus-again-lifts-auckland-restrictions

22. Liam O'Dell, "Jacinda Ardern Admits New Zealand Will Become a Two-Tier Society between Vaccinated and Unvaccinated," *The Independent*, October 25, 2021, https://www.independent.co.uk/tv/news/new-zealand-jacinda-ardern-coronavirus-vaccines-ve5572e26.

23. "German Health Minister to Public: Pandemic Is Not Over," *VOA News*, March 11, 2022, https://www.voanews.com/a/german-health-minister-to-public-pandemic-is-not-over-/6481305.html.

24. Ayhan Simsek, "Vaccines Are the Way out of Pandemic, Says German Chancellor," *Anadolu Agency*, December 31, 2021, https://www.aa.com.tr/en/europe/vaccines-are-the-way-out-of-pandemic-says-german-chancellor/2462328.

25. Chico Harlan and Mia Alberti, Portugal Has Nearly Run out of People to Vaccinate. What Comes Next," *The Washington Post*, September 30, 2021, https://www.washingtonpost.com/world/2021/09/30/portugal-vaccination-covid/.

26. "Portugal Adopts New Restrictive Measures despite High Vaccination Rate," *Euractiv*, November 26, 2021, https://www.euractiv.com/section/coronavirus/news/portugal-

adopts-new-restrictive-measures-despite-high-vaccination-
rate/.

27. Natasha Donn, "Portugal Still Running with Highest Covid
    Case Count in Europe," *Portugal Resident,* June 8, 2022,
    https://www.portugalresident.com/portugal-still-running-
    with-highest-covid-case-count-in-europe/.

28. A. Odysseus Patrick, "Australia Has Almost Eliminated the
    Coronavirus - by Putting Faith in Science," *The Washington Post,*
    November 5, 2020, https://www.washing-
    tonpost.com/world/asia_pacific/australia-coronavirus-cases-
    melbourne-lockdown/2020/11/05/96c198b2-1cb7-11eb-ad53-
    4c1fda49907d_story.html.

29. "Hong Kong Reports 56,827 COVID-19 Cases, New Record
    Daily High," *Reuters,* March 3, 2022, https://www.reu-
    ters.com/business/healthcare-pharmaceuticals/hong-kong-re-
    ports-56827-covid-19-cases-new-record-daily-high-2022-03-03/.

30. Eileen AJ Connelly, "New York Reports over 90,000 COVID
    Cases to Break Another State Record," *New York Post,* January
    8, 2022, https://nypost.com/2022/01/08/positive-covid-cases-
    top-90000-across-new-york-for-first-time/.

31. "COVID-19: Data," New York City Department of Health and
    Mental Hygiene, accessed August 1, 2022,
    https://www1.nyc.gov/site/doh/covid/covid-19-data-to-
    tals.page.

32. "Coronavirus in the U.S.: Latest Map and Case Count," *The
    New York Times,* accessed March 3, 2020, https://www.ny-
    times.com/interactive/2021/us/covid-cases.html.

33. Ibid.

34. Ibid.

35. Ibid.

CHAPTER 9. SEEDS OF HOPE

1. Nestor Makhno, *The Struggle Against the State and Other Essays*, ed. Alexandre Sirda, trans. Paul Sharkey (Oakland, California: AK Press), 45.

2. "COVID-19 Media Conference — 29 November 2021 at 4pm," Unite against COVID-19, last modified November 30, 2021, https://covid19.govt.nz/news-and-data/latest-news/covid-19-media-conference-29-november-2021/.

3. Ibid.

4. Ludwig von Mises, *Liberty and Property* (Auburn, Alabama: Ludwig von Mises Institute, 2009), 32.

CHAPTER 10. FINAL THOUGHTS

1. Humphrey Carpenter and Christopher Tolkien, *The Letters of J. R. R. Tolkien* (London: George Allen & Unwin, 1981), 52.

www.ingramcontent.com/pod-product-compliance
Lightning Source LLC
Chambersburg PA
CBHW021535260326
41914CB00001B/27